Making a Difference

Making a Difference

Eleven Inspiring Difference Makers

MARGARET ATTWOOD

Foreword by Andrew Taylor

RESOURCE *Publications* · Eugene, Oregon

MAKING A DIFFERENCE
Eleven Inspiring Difference Makers

Resource Publications
An Imprint of Wipf and Stock Publishers
199 W. 8th Ave., Suite 3
Eugene, OR 97401

www.wipfandstock.com

PAPERBACK ISBN: 979-8-3852-7078-1
HARDCOVER ISBN: 979-8-3852-7079-8
EBOOK ISBN: 979-8-3852-7080-4

VERSION NUMBER 02/17/26

Contents

Foreword

I am honored to endorse *Making a Difference* by Margaret Attwood, an insightful and inspiring exploration of leadership that examines how individuals can shape their communities through courage, faith, and purpose.

This book features a range of impactful leaders, including my wife, Carolyn Taylor, whose steadfast faith and commitment have driven transformative change. It also highlights Tim Costello, a globally recognized advocate for justice and equity, whose leadership is rooted in compassion and a deep sense of moral responsibility. Tim's ability to challenge systems of inequality while building bridges across diverse communities underscores the importance of leading with both conviction and empathy in today's complex world.

Equally compelling is the story of Jean-Paul Samputu, whose journey of forgiveness after the Rwandan genocide offers a moving testament to the resilience of the human spirit. Jean-Paul's decision to embrace forgiveness rather than bitterness transformed not only his own life but also the lives of those he has touched through his advocacy for reconciliation and healing. His story exemplifies how leadership grounded in grace can rebuild broken communities and inspire hope in the face of profound suffering.

What sets *Making a Difference* apart is its structured framework, which weaves these personal stories into broader leadership themes informed by expert research. Margaret masterfully connects the real-world experiences of these leaders to universal principles such as resilience, collaboration, and the courage to challenge the status quo. By doing so, the book goes beyond storytelling, offering a practical lens for understanding what it takes to lead with integrity and purpose.

This integration of narrative and research ensures the book is both relatable and deeply thought provoking. *Making a Difference* serves as a bridge between theory and practice, equipping leaders at all levels with tools to navigate challenges while staying true to their values.

I highly recommend *Making a Difference* as an invaluable resource for anyone seeking inspiration, guidance, and a deeper understanding of how to lead with purpose and leave a lasting legacy.

Andrew Taylor
General Manager
New Peninsula Community Caring Inc.

About the Author

Margaret draws on her experience as a social worker, social researcher, Management Course facilitator, and business coach to move into the interviewees' world and explore their personal motivation. A member of the Peninsula Writers Club, she has written extensively on her own experiences following separation, *From Chrysalis to Butterfly*, and creating a blended family, *Enriching the Blended Family*. As a journaler, she is passionate about people sharing their own stories and empowering others. She found the experience of meeting and interviewing the eleven people cameoed in her book both inspiring and uplifting. Her Christian faith provides an empowering context for her own life and passion to make a difference.

Margaret is married and lives with her husband, Peter, in Mount Martha, Victoria. She has four children and eight grandchildren. As well as being a writer, she loves sewing clothing and gifts, learning french, walking and exercising daily and living by the beach, and enjoys a wide network of friends. She is an active member of New Peninsula Baptist Church, Mount Martha.

Acknowledgements

My journey with this book has extended over 14 years and it has been a series of small miracles. The interview process was very organic and each person I interviewed inspired me to meet someone else and develop the conversation further. I do want to thank the eleven people cameoed, for their inspiration: Tim Costello, Duncan Brown, Lydia Harb, Jean-Paul Samputu, Helen Macnaughtan, Julie Parke, Katherine Barling, Cas Taylor and Jamie Edgerton and also acknowledge both Russell and Anne Costello who passed away in 2016 and 2022 respectively.

The acceptance by Wipf and Stock was another small miracle and I'd like to thank the staff team of Matt Wimer, Emily Callihan, George Callihan, Andrew Jacobs, Hannah Starr, Joe Delany, and Kyle Lundurg for their very professional and consultative input. They all assisted in the further miracle of getting the manuscript to publication quality.

Suan Lee Campbell and Sarah Bacaller gave excellent feedback and review in the early copy-editing, and I received feedback and advice from Jeanette Woods, Muriel Cooper Gillian Fulcher and David Reitveld and Mark Matthews. I have also appreciated the support and encouragement from Paul Crothers, Lucy Kenshole, Andrew Taylor and Glenda Holbrook and their willingness to endorse my work.

My family have been a great support during the book's journey. Tommy McCubbin has helped greatly with social media and the marketing process and Alicia Visini for her assistance with video production. Sarah McCubbin and Rebecca McCubbin have been encouraging and supportive and Peter my husband has been a wonderful support and encourager through the various stages of the process. I feel the Lord has been there with me creating the small miracles on the pathway forward.

1

Exploring the Context
of Making a Difference

THE BOOK IS ABOUT exploring what motivates us to make a difference with others. Most people do want to contribute to others, but what causes some people to do extraordinary things, to move beyond their immediate circle, to contribute to a broader or global community? In interviewing a range of people who have inspired me, I tease out the factors that distinguish their motivation to contribute. Do we play a small or a significant game, or are we discouraged by facing obstacles? I explore how we can use these distinctions to get in touch with our passion, expand our view of ourselves, identify our values, overcome any obstacles, and really make a difference.

WHAT DO I MEAN BY "MAKING A DIFFERENCE"?

Life is no brief candle to me: it is a sort of splendid torch which I have got hold of for the moment, and I want to make it burn as brightly as possible before handing it on to future generations.[1]

1. Henderson, *George Bernard Shaw*, 512.

When I was young, I did feel quite invincible. I would dream of flying—rising into the air, over roofs and trees to escape danger. As I grew into adolescence my confidence eroded, and I began to wonder if I could make a difference. I was interested in having a world where people lived in peace and no one went hungry. How could I, as one individual, really impact that dream? I gave up on it for some time.

Making a difference is essentially about contributing to others in a powerful way. It is moving beyond our focus on self, our own needs and desires, to looking outwards. It is being a transformational leader in showing respect, empathy, creativity, and inspiration for a vision and influencing others to share or support our passion for that vision.

It is being motivated by core values (Christian, spiritual, or ethical), rather than self-interest, and going above and beyond what is required or expected by community norms.

Psychologist and educator Jordan Peterson offers some fascinating guidelines for a successful life, and four particularly resonated with the idea of "making a difference."[2]

The key "rules" that relate to making a difference were "stand up straight with your shoulders back," "compare yourself with who you were yesterday, not who someone else is today," "pursue what is meaningful" (not expedient), and "tell the truth."[3] Even though Peterson identifies rules for living that are expressed in terms of behavior, behind these are core values that inform and drive the behavior.

Let us look at these further. In focusing on *standing up straight with your shoulders back*, he is encouraging self-respect, pride, and confidence. *Comparing yourself with your earlier self rather than others* suggests self-growth and development, setting goals and direction, and taking responsibility for your life's journey. To *pursue what is meaningful (rather than expedient)* implies goal setting again, identifying core values and a focus on the greater good.

2. Peterson, *12 Rules for Life.*
3. Peterson, *12 Rules for Life,* 1, 85, 161, 202.

What is "meaningful"? Peterson suggests that "meaning is the way, the path of life more abundant, the place you live when you are guided by love and speaking truth, and when nothing you want or could possibly want takes precedence."[4]

In further elaborating on what is meaningful, Jordan Peterson suggests that "the soul of the individual eternally hungers for the heroism of genuine Being, and that the willingness to take on the responsibility is identical to the decision to live a meaningful life. If we each live properly, we will collectively flourish."[5] The fourth rule, "tell the truth," is about honesty, ethics, being open and authentic with yourself, and tapping into your dream and what you really want to accomplish in life.

Who we are being is a key concept to explore in creating a context for making a difference. It is useful to distinguish *being* from *doing* and *having*, which tend to get a lot more air space and far greater focus in our current culture. For example, I might be driven by what I want to *have* and what I can *do* in order that I may *be* someone. However, a more powerful sequence is to start from *being* and move to *doing* and then *having*.

Who am I being? How am I communicating, and what is the quality of my relationships? Are my relationships singing? Have I accepted mediocrity? Have I given up on making a difference to that family member, friend, neighbor? *Who I am being* is impacted by my ability to listen, to be with and to be present to those whom I care about, accepting what is so and acknowledging those around me for who they are. *Being* is also about the place where you are coming from: the context of your contribution. This touches on your core values about what you are giving or what you can get back—the "in order to." Do we put a higher value on selfless giving? One assumes giving is a selfless commitment, but what is in it for you?

What I am doing should flow from whom I am being. Doing is about *being in action*. Is my contribution in the domain of "doing"? Do I enjoy doing things for others: shopping for my neighbor, caring for my grandchildren, giving a gift to a friend, coaching the

4. Peterson, *12 Rules for Life*, 201.

5. Peterson, *12 Rules for Life*, 201.

local hockey team? Is *doing* a strong aspect of my profession? Am I a performer expressing my creativity through dance? Or music? Am I a keyhole surgeon, or the committed educator, developing the next generation?

Having also flows through from being and doing. Having is associated with material possessions, which is a strong driver in our culture. But *having* in this context is about qualities as well as resources. Do you have the tenacity and commitment to follow through? Do you make a difference through having wealth, having outstanding qualities, or resources? Do you have skills, talents, or resources to share with others? Personal attributes or resources can be used to make a difference to others. Do you have inspiring relationships? Do you make a difference in your interactions, through listening, sharing, empathy? Do you have a fulfilling career? Do you have a satisfying and challenging life journey?

CONTEXT AND FRAMING

One question to consider is the *context* of making a difference. The context is the setting of an event, the circumstances, and the background that determine the meaning of an event and enable you to understand it. In contrast, *framing* is the process of defining the context or issues surrounding an event in a way that serves to influence how the context or issues are perceived and evaluated. Context is the bigger picture, while framing is more discretionary.

I started this book really putting a higher value on those whose context is wider and who impact many people at a community or global level. But others make a difference one person at a time, or to one person specifically. I am reminded of Katherine, one of the people I interviewed, who gave up her job to take care of her autistic nephew and really gave him love and a series of coping skills so he was able to handle social situations more effectively and appropriately. Julie fostered a disabled child and gave her the parents she needed. So the breadth of social impact is important, but everyone's contribution is of value.

Contribution can push us outside our comfort zone in terms of the environment in which we contribute, the financial commitment, or the time requirement. Is this another measure of the value?

Contribution can be made through our vocation or through our interests outside work.

Certainly, in choosing a career we can be motivated by "making a difference" or contributing to others. The community places a high value on this; however, in this book I am looking beyond this to what we often do outside our career—where we aren't necessarily paid but put time and energy into a cause that benefits others.

Do people want to make a difference? I do see the world as a positive, optimistic place. People want to belong, be accepted, and contribute but don't always know how or even where to start. Maybe in providing role models, opportunities, and ideas, it will help others move down the pathway to fulfillment.

Contribution often comes at a cost. Tim Costello moved from the eastern suburbs of Melbourne to inner-city St Kilda with his young family; missionaries and qualified professionals, such as those who work with Médicins Sans Frontières, move to places of cultural difference and economic and social restrictions, often exposing themselves to danger. The "calling" or commitment is the motivation to step outside what we know or are comfortable doing. In my earlier voluntary work mentoring mothers with COACH, a local family support program, I was confronted by how others live in terms of order, cleanliness, beauty, and serenity. There were often clothes and toys everywhere, piles in the corner, passages blocked with dirty clothes, and the sink and kitchen benches overflowing with dirty dishes. Despite this being challenging, I do accept the differences, not being judgmental, critical, or offering advice but simply listening and giving them supportive feedback so they feel valued, appreciated, and worthy. My context is empowerment and commitment through the mentoring role. This then impacts the quality of their mothering, their emotional wellbeing and ability to regain stability after an upset or work through things themselves.

I've often thought about contribution in terms of concentric circles.[6] You are in the center, surrounded by family and friends, then communities, our country, the region, and the world. How broad is your scope and playing field? How far does your passion, commitment, skill and knowledge, and persistence spread? How many people do you touch?

I am asserting that everyone wants to make a difference in their own lives and in the lives of others. We choose different playing fields: our family, our community, our nation, and the world. The bigger the game, the more challenging and riskier it is. The higher the stakes, the greater the demand for energy and commitment.

A question to ask ourselves is, Am I playing small or playing full-on, like my life depends on it? We choose the scope of our game. Can I expand the kaleidoscope of my self-expression and contribution?

Former US president John F. Kennedy created a powerful context for contribution when he said, "Ask not what your country can do for you—ask what you can do for your country."[7]

Ian Hickingbotham's book *Waiting for the Tide* is a wonderful stream of consciousness writing, following his journey through excruciating back pain and being required to lie on his back for six weeks.[8] As a Christian minister, the journey tested his faith. One of Hickingbotham's chapters is on "framing," a very powerful neurolinguistic distinction. He quotes from a beautiful poem titled "Outwitted" by Edwin Markam:

> He drew a circle and shut me out,
> Heretic, rebel a thing to flout,
> But love and I had a wit to win,
> We drew a circle that took him in.[9]

---

6. See appendix 1, "Circles of Self-Expression and Contribution."

7. John Fitzgerald Kennedy became US president in 1961. This quote was part of his inaugural address in January 1961 when he became the thirty-fifth president of the USA. See Kennedy, "Inaugural Address."

8. Hickingbotham, *Waiting for the Tide.*

9. Markham, *Shoes of Happiness,* 2.

The concept of framing is useful as it creates a context from which to operate. *Making a Difference* is about exploring or uncovering our context, our frame. Are you committed to contributing to your family, the wider community, or is your context a global one? Framing also touches on values and beliefs. If your values context is "interconnectedness," everyone made in the likeness of God, then there is no separation, and your context is not "selective" but "universal."

"There but for the grace of God, goes John Bradford."[10] This is a phrase that reminds us of our "oneness." Context framing is also important in our view of ourselves. Do we envision ourselves bigger than we know ourselves to be? Werner Erhard, who founded the Est training in the 1970s which later became Landmark Education, spoke about the power of creating a "big game," or a context that is like throwing our hat over a high wall, so that we must stretch and think creatively or expansively to retrieve it.[11] It also means that we close the "back door" so we haven't a way out. Our mindset about ourselves and others is shaped by our values but gives us the choice or freedom to select our pathway in life. Is your pathway going to be satisfying your material desires, and self-interest, or looking at what you can do in the world to "make a difference" and leave a legacy?

Think about how would you like to be remembered. What is your legacy? Another powerful question to consider is, Are you willing to give up who you are for whom you could become?

Who we are for ourselves and our family can ripple out and impact wider circles. We need to start with what's close and who we are being in these relationships. Our basic values and life context,

10. This quote is from John Bradford, reportedly said in 1553 when he saw criminals being led to their execution. He himself was executed two years later for heresy, as a Protestant in then–Roman Catholic England. Bickersteth, *Treatise on Prayer*, 60.

11. Werner Erhard, an American born in 1935, established Est training in 1971, which became The Forum in 1985 and Landmark Education in 1991. Millions of people around the world have participated in these personal development programs. Erhard wrote several books, including *Celebrating Relationships* and *The Heart of the Matter*. William Warren Bartley III wrote about him in *Werner Erhard: The Transformation of a Man*.

or frame, shape who we are being. I have identified that love, acceptance, and contribution are my central core values.

What would it take to have the same level of commitment to our neighbor as to our family? I have always loved the distinction "interconnectedness," acknowledging that we are all interdependent. I could be the poverty-stricken mother in Africa, the dispossessed refugee family, the homeless widow. Our similarities are stronger than our differences, and the biblical verse "We know that in everything God works for good with those who love him" (Rom 8:28) underscores this.

My paternal grandmother, Maggie, was widowed at thirty-eight, with six small children ranging in age from two to twelve years old. Richard, her husband, died from the Spanish flu in 1918; he had been managing their family drapery business in a Victorian country town. Maggie struggled to look after the children and keep the family together after her husband's death. This verse was on the wall of my father's bedroom as a child, and I have always been inspired that Maggie, his mother, was able to see the world through such uplifting eyes, or such a powerful context.

SELF-IMAGE, SELF-AWARENESS, AND MINDSET

It is important to step back and reflect on who we are and what we know about ourselves.

Despite my early altruism, I did begin to question what I could do as one individual.

Through participating in a personal development program in my late thirties (Landmark Education), I was able to reframe my context and see that my belief and commitment to impacting these things that were important to me was the key ingredient. Knowing I could act was the platform from which I started. I joined The Hunger Project (THP) and began fundraising and supported the actions and initiatives they took to end hunger.[12] At this time, it

12. The Hunger Project is a global movement established in the USA in 1977 and in Australia in 1983. Its goal is to end world hunger. It sees the people living in hunger as the solution, not the problem, and through its Vision, Commitment, and Action workshops, it has empowered thousands of grassroots

was an impossible and idealistic dream, but by 2010, there had been significant improvements in reducing the number of people in the world who had chronic persistent hunger, and the UN Millennium Development goals were established.[13] The Hunger Project's commitment was that by 2030 hunger will be ended on the planet. The program of The Hunger Project empowers hungry people, particularly women, to be the solution to end their hunger, not the problem to address. Through the Vision, Commitment, and Action workshops, held in local villages in Africa and India, they focus on the issues that are the most important for them to resolve at a village level: safe drinking water, health services, sanitation, and education.

In 2016, I took on the challenge of generating $5,000 for The Hunger Project, the base amount required to become a global investor. I had considered it over the past decade, but each time I had decided it was out of reach. In 2016, I decided it was now or never. I started to think creatively about ways to generate funds and, through several sponsored walks and a lunch, raised $3,800. I fell short of my goal of $5,000, but I did achieve a lot more than I had ever done in a year. I empowered others to support me through inspiring them with this global goal and, in doing so, got to recreate who I knew myself to be.

So, what factors shape our view of ourselves and what we feel we could or couldn't achieve in life?

Our family background and culture have a significant impact on the conversations we have about ourselves. Were we encouraged and supported as children or criticized and humiliated? My experience certainly was one of encouragement and being given

---

people in India and Africa to end hunger in their villages. See www.thp.org for more information.

13. The Millennium Development Goals (MDGs), established in 2000, focused primarily on addressing poverty, hunger, and basic human development in developing countries, with eight goals and twenty-one targets. In 2015, the Sustainable Development Goals (SDGs) were adopted by all UN member states, expanding the agenda to seventeen goals and 169 targets, covering a broader range of issues including economic growth, social inclusion, and environmental protection, and applying to all countries worldwide. See United Nations, "Millenium Development Goals" and "Transforming Our World."

opportunities such as calisthenics, swimming, and music, where I could develop skills, overcome challenges, and gain a sense of accomplishment and worth. Growing up in a family culture, values and attitudes are imbibed, so we take them on board. That's just the way things are. A friend indicated that he was always criticized and belittled growing up, so he took on board that he wasn't okay, and this was reflected in the way he led his life, not allowing people to get close to him, being angry and aggressive to protect himself from being hurt.

As we grow up and complete our education, we learn to look more objectively at ourselves and our early influences, and we become more self-aware. Dr. Eric Berne, through his studies, has identified three ego states which influence how we operate: the child, the parent, and the adult.[14]

When in the child state (during the first five years of life) we take things on board unquestioningly. This phase is about emotions and how we feel; we are often very impulsive and want immediate gratification. The parent state, which also we imbibe in the first five years, is about what we are taught: rules, requirements, dos, and don'ts. The third state, the adult state, is when we start to look objectively at the first two states and develop an emotional maturity, realizing that what we took on board is not the "truth" but a perception, which may or may not be so. We start to see what works and doesn't work. Having a tantrum when things don't go our way is a child's way of responding, but at forty it doesn't always have a positive impact. Telling our staff what to do, in the parent mode, may get a short-term result, but we don't get their emotional buy-in or commitment to the task, as they don't have to take responsibility.

The other aspect of self-awareness is recognizing your strengths and areas which could be developed further. You may have grown up in a very judgmental household, but in the adult state you see that you don't need to continue those attitudes or behaviors. You can choose to stay above the line, with a glass-half-full approach. We also are more attuned to our impact on others.

14. Berne, *Games People Play.*

Being very spontaneous and effervescent may work well socially, but quieter people become intimidated and close down. Maybe the extrovert needs to temper their enthusiasm with active listening and observing.

So, what is the view I have of myself? Am I confident of success? Do I persist if I come across challenges or give up when it gets too hard? Do I ask for support or try and do things on my own?

Self-awareness is about understanding our values and the frame in which we view ourselves. If we notice we get deterred easily from our focus, maybe we can change this? Do I blame others if I am not successful, or do I take full responsibility myself?

Self-awareness, self-management, social awareness, and relationship management are the four facets of emotional intelligence, and the key to emotional maturity.[15]

DIRECTION, GOAL SETTING,
AND RESPONSIBILITY

Another aspect we need to consider is our direction. Do we have goals to accomplish? What are we building? What do we want to achieve in life?

Goal setting and deciding what we want to accomplish can be very useful. It does involve writing our goal down and considering the time frame and process so the idea becomes grounded. Measurability in terms of outcomes and time frames gives us a pathway to follow. Consideration of the obstacles and roadblocks can also help us prepare for and address these challenges. Identifying the benefits can also be important if you are wanting to motivate yourself and others.

Do we play small and set a goal that we can easily achieve or go for a stretch goal that we don't know how to achieve? A hairy audacious goal![16]

15. See Goleman, *Emotional Intelligence*. The author is an internationally known psychologist; over five million copies of the book mentioned here have been sold, and it has been translated into forty languages. See his website at www.danielgoleman.info.

16. A 'big hairy audacious goal' was a term introduced by Jim Collins and

Being a writer is a stretch goal for me. I love the flow and creativity of writing; however, when I think about publishing, a few considerations create obstacles.

What if I am knocked back numerous times? What if readers aren't interested in my topic? Nonsense! If I believe in myself and what I want to share, I will accomplish my goal.

Do we need to let go of old conversations and self-talk and mindsets that hold us back?

Are you willing to give up who you are for whom you could become?

This is the framework for moving forward—knowing who you are, accepting your strengths and capabilities and those aspects that let you down. Can you overcome the inevitable obstacles to achieve your goal?

Responsibility can be interpreted as "the ability to choose our response."[17] As mature adults, we take responsibility for ourselves, and our families, but how much further does our commitment to be responsible extend?

Do we take responsibility for our environment? How far does our responsibility extend in terms of our driving, our environmental footprint, our energy usage? In order to take responsibility, we need to value ourselves, have self-worth, and feel whole and complete. Responsibility also relates again to our core values. As a Christian, I want to live a life of contribution, expressing God's love and empowering others.

Does taking responsibility extend to social justice? Ensuring others have a right to legal, educational, and housing opportunities? What about global issues, issues of environmental sustainability, access to food and water, and basic standards of living? The political arena is another area where people take responsibility and make a difference. The performing arts, again, is about contribution to our quality of life, entertainment, and pleasure.

Jerry Porras in their book *Built to Last: Successful Habits of Visionary Companies.*

17. Covey, *7 Habits*, 71.

DISTINGUISHING OUR CORE VALUES

Who we are being, what we do, and how we share what we have all emanates from our core values. Core values are principles or beliefs that a person, group, or organization views as being centrally important to their actions, decisions, and identity. I wanted to distinguish mine to get a sense of how they have driven my passion.

Love. Relationships and reconciliation, respect and empathy.

Faith. Trust and belief in God (in a greater being), belief in the goodness of others.

Integrity. This is about basic honesty in word and deed and, at its highest level, being true to yourself.

Contribution. Doing things for others, thinking about their needs, sharing with others.

Creativity. Self-expression, sharing your skills and talents with others.

Choice. Having the means to make choices. Being willing to choose.

Acceptance. Having understanding, respect, empathy, curiosity to understand and accept others. Not being judgmental.

Forgiveness. This emanates from love and acceptance. Being willing to forgive others for actions or words.

Communication. Expressing love, acknowledgment, working through issues, being proactive. Listening and being present.

Interconnectedness. Focusing on similarities, respect and acceptance of differences.

Passion. Having the energy and commitment to immerse oneself in the path we choose and sustain that commitment.

David Suzuki's book on the sacred balance extends the values conversation, including sustainability, the sacredness of life, being custodians not owners, intergenerational responsibility, and interconnectedness.[18] Other core values at the interpersonal level are a

18. Suzuki, *Sacred Balance.* David Suzuki, a Japanese Canadian born in

focus on others, being responsible, optimism, authentic speaking, and collaboration.

When talking about love, Krishnamurti, an Indian philosopher and mystic, said, "To love is not to ask anything in return, not even to feel you are giving something, and it is only such love that can know freedom."[19]

The Bible also has a strong focus on love as the foundation of who we are being: "Let brotherly love continue. Do not neglect to show hospitality to strangers" (Heb 13:1–2); "Do not neglect to do good and share what you have" (Heb 13:16); "This is my commandment, that you love one another as I have loved you" (John 15:12).

This really points to the focus being contribution rather than self-interest.

M. Scott Peck in the *Road Less Traveled* suggests that choosing a special, or challenging, path free from conformity is how we make a difference.[20] In another book, *The Different Drum*, he suggests that the overall purpose of communication is reconciliation, and this in turn leads to love and harmony. "We are all called to be peacemakers and as peacemakers, called to community. One of the things about a 'calling' is to be an individual of integrity, and this often means to speak out."[21] Your leadership will impact others. Walking to the beat of a "different drum" leads to changing the rules of human communication and selling the world on love.

1936, is a geneticist, broadcaster, and environmental activist. He has authored or co-authored over fifty books and hosted several environmental TV series including *The Nature of Things*, which he hosted for forty-four years.

19. Krishnamurti, *Think on These Things*, 19. Born in India (1895–1986), Jiddu Krishnamurti was a philosopher, speaker, and writer. He was raised to be the prophesied World Teacher, an advanced position in the theosophical tradition, but later rejected that mantle and disbanded the organization set up for that purpose. Throughout his life, he wrote many books and stressed the need for a revolution in the psyche of every human, insisting that true change arises not from external systems or beliefs but from individual self-understanding. See Foundation Staff, "Krishnamurti's Biography."

20. Peck, *Road Less Traveled*. This book encourages the reader to act independently, freeing themselves from the conformity of others.

21. Peck, *Different Drum*, 329.

WHAT MOTIVATES US TO TAKE ACTION?

In *Walking in the World* Marjorie Von Harten talks about anger or outrage as a source of creative inspiration.[22] On reflection in my journal, these are the areas that stirred my anger:

- Climate change and our environment and the urgency of action

- Hunger and inequality: inequity of resources and opportunity

- The charade of politics: from altruism to self-interest

- People not being passionate about life: apathy and indifference

- Wastage and extravagant materialism

- Persecution of others for their beliefs and devaluation of spiritual beliefs

In the last ten years there have been several changes that have impacted my anger: the rise of ISIS and their brutality; the conflict in Syria, with so many people dispossessed and having to flee; the Hasad leadership being more concerned about their own power than their people; and Australia's own immigration policy and attitude to asylum seekers. The United Nations Human Rights Council has been critical of Australia's treatment of refugees, and the government's focus on preventing refugee traffickers and turning back the refugee boats is a justification for an inhumane policy. In the 2022 federal election, the Liberal Party lost power to the Labor Party, and the policy was relaxed. The plight of Indigenous Australians and the disappointing outcomes from significant financial allocations, but also more recently the lack of unity on Australia's proposed 2023 Indigenous Voice referendum, is very frustrating.[23]

So, anger can be a motivation to act. Maybe it is about channelling anger into passion. However, I am more interested in the motive of love. Maybe anger is the flip side of the love?

22. Von Harten, *Walking in the World*.

23. Note: As this book was written initially in 2023, some of the more recent current affairs, both globally and locally, are not covered here.

I want to do something, but what? What am I called to do? How effective will I be?

In *Man and Superman: A Comedy and a Philosophy*, George Bernard Shaw addressed both motivation and context, writing,

> This is the true joy of life, the being used for a purpose recognized by yourself as a mighty one; . . . the being a force of nature instead of a feverish, selfish little clod of ailments and grievances, complaining that the world will not devote itself to making you happy.[24]

In Shaw's "Art and Money" speech, he also stated, "I am of the opinion that my life belongs to the whole community, and as long as I live, it is my privilege to do for it whatever I can."[25]

Is contribution related to life phases? At certain points in our lives, we need a greater focus inward, or on smaller concentric circles—dependent children, sick family member, elderly parent. Maybe in serving others, we show what is best for the family. Maybe, it is who we *are being* in the world, regardless of the circumstances or life stage.

MOTIVATION AND VALUE BASE

Some people are motivated to do something for others; our inter-connectedness means that they want to serve others. Certainly, when we think back to some of the motivations of the last century, with people traveling to new lands, the goal was about "converting" them to Christianity, imposing their values on others rather than understanding and respecting the other. In terms of a values clash, I'm reminded of Australia's Stolen Generations, where people of Aboriginal descent were forcibly taken from their families and placed in non-Aboriginal contexts, with the goal of enculturating them into "white society." Taking children away to a "better home," the authorities wanted to impact the situation, but

24. Shaw, *Man and Superman*, xxxii ("To Arthur Bingham Walkley").
25. Henderson, *George Bernard Shaw*, 512.

based on flawed values, they caused untold generational damage, distress, and sadness.

Maslow's hierarchy of needs, developed as part of his theory of motivation, gives us a useful framework for understanding motivation.[26] According to Maslow, base-level motivations focus on addressing basic needs, such as finding or providing food or shelter.

Maslow's hierarchy is also of value in enabling us to think about our view of ourselves. When we are struggling to meet basic needs, then it is very difficult to focus on others and how we can contribute. For some in the caring professions, motivation is about relationships, helping people to heal relationships. At Maslow's level of self-actualization, people are motivated to contribute to others, given that the more basic needs of food, security, and relationship fulfillment have been met.

Marianne Williamson very poignantly suggests that "our deepest fear is that we are powerful beyond measure" rather than our fear being feelings of inadequacy.[27] We are all "meant to shine" and "manifest the glory of God"; "playing small doesn't serve the world."[28] Through our example we inspire others and are freed from our fears.

Why do we play small? Research professor and author Brené Brown, known for best-selling books such as *Atlas of the Heart* and *Daring Greatly*, suggests that we play small because of our fear of being vulnerable and taking risks.[29] We prefer to look good and play safe and often disconnect. She encourages us to build up our "shame resilience" through "recognizing shame (in relation to our body, parenting, money)" and by "understanding the triggers, practicing critical awareness, reaching out and connecting with others."[30] Sharing about our feelings of shame is also important.[31]

---

26. Maslow, "Theory of Human Motivation." See the hierarchy of needs in appendix 2.

27. Williamson, *Return to Love*, 190.

28. Williamson, *Return to Love*, 190.

29. Brown, *Daring Greatly*.

30. Brown, *Daring Greatly*, 73.

31. Brown, *Daring Greatly*, 73.

W. H. Murray, who led the 1951 Scottish Himalayan expedition, saw motivation as committing and the power that arises and generates "a whole stream of events" from being bold and making a commitment.[32]

> Until one is committed, there is hesitancy, the chance to draw back, always ineffectiveness. Concerning all acts of initiative (and creation), there is one elementary truth the ignorance of which kills countless ideas and splendid plans: that the moment one definitely commits oneself, the providence moves too. A whole stream of events issues from the decision, raising in one's favor all manner of unforeseen incidents, meetings, and material assistance, which no man could have dreamt would have come his way. I learned a deep respect for one of Goethe's couplets:
> "Whatever you can do or dream you can, begin it.
> Boldness has genius, power, and magic in it!"[33]

In terms of using our talents or abilities, should we be considering the relative value of impacting just a few people as compared to impacting a whole community? Is doing something in our own environment of greater value than serving overseas? Tim Costello's scope and reach is global, impacting many people in our own country, as well as those whom World Vision works with in the majority world. Is that of more value than Katherine giving up her work to spend time with and nurture her autistic nephew? I'm not sure that putting a value on the breadth of contribution is appropriate.

If what you choose to do is using your talents and abilities, if those to whom you contribute gain value and you judge your actions to be worthwhile, or you help to meet community values or express integrity, goodness, and equity in empowering others, then you make a difference.

32. Murray, *Scottish Himalayan Expedition*, 7.
33. Murray, *Scottish Himalayan Expedition*, 7.

Making a Difference

Being in the moment,
Enjoying every interaction,
Is making a difference.
Expressing and sharing what we are experiencing,
Reflecting on what occurs,
The impact, the feelings,
Gives a window into our lives and allows others to access
theirs.
I am the possibility of abundance and contribution
And presence this in my sharing.
People are courageous and inventive,
Adaptable and loving.
Do they know themselves in this way?
So, we are also a mirror
Reflecting back to others their greatness.
Being in life is choosing . . .
The path of empowerment and joy,
And contribution is so expansive and infectious
It returns to us in abundance.
Seeing ourselves bigger
Than we know ourselves to be,
Believing and committing to change
And seeing it through to the end,
To its completion,
Is really making a difference.
Whether it be sustainability, peace, ending poverty and
hunger,
Visiting a neighbor, walking for medical research,
The focus is out there,
Beyond our parameters to a wider context.
The obstacles and pull of our own needs
Will be ever-present.
It is acknowledging them, rising above them,
Not getting sucked back into playing small
And rationalizing our inaction.
It is tapping into our passion,
Areas of strength,
Being open to what God wants us to do,
Following that and sharing that with others

Making a Difference

So it becomes a bigger game,
Raising the stakes.
In a big game the question often is
Do I start? or Where do I start?
It is about starting conversations,
Birthing the dream,
Taking small steps
But never losing sight of the bigger picture.
The conversation forms a map,
A patchwork of ideas and resources
On which to build and give away to others.
A big game is risky.
Am I willing to fail?
To give it my all and not achieve my goal?
We don't want to be immobilized in inaction.
Being true to our values,
Networking and collaborating with kindred spirits
Relying on God's grace
Builds a strong foundation
On which others can stand
And expand the dream
Into a new realm of creativity and freedom.

2

Eleven Inspiring Difference Makers

I HAVE INTERVIEWED ELEVEN people who inspired me with their actions and explored what has motivated them to go beyond what most people would do. Quite a number of those interviewed were motivated by their Christian values, to make a difference through their unique abilities and show God's love in their communities. Others were motivated by their family situation or their own need to contribute to others. In my conversations with them I explore what enabled them to take on significant projects and go above and beyond to achieve their results.

Several of the people interviewed have high profiles, while others are ordinary people expressing their passion through significant projects. Most are people with whom you and I can identify and take inspiration from; they are just like us.

RUSSELL AND ANNE COSTELLO

May 20, 2012
Coronella Retirement Village, Nunawading, Australia

Russell and Anne were old family friends through Hyde Park Methodist Church in Kew, and they were a couple whom I greatly admired, so I was interested to get a sense of what motivated Russell particularly to do what he did in his life.

I met with Russell and Anne after a concert at their facility and conducted an interview over about an hour and a half. Russell is quite frail at ninety-one and is confined to a wheelchair. He moved from his and Anne's independent unit to supported accommodation nearby in the same complex. He has a beautiful melodic voice, and even though it is getting softer, it is very calm and re-assuring. Anne is livelier and more self-expressed; however, Russell has a great sense of humor, and our session was punctuated with peals of laughter and delightful reminiscences.

On one of our families' Seaford holidays together, Anne, Russell, my parents, and Julie—my sister—and I were playing in the shallows. Suddenly, Anne jumped into Russell's arms because a crab had bitten her toe. The next moment they both collapsed in the water when Russell was bitten as well, followed by much laughter! Both their memories are fantastic, with Anne sometimes adding or correcting Russell's reflections. She also recalled things about our upbringing and parents that I had forgotten.

"Your father was a stickler for you girls chewing your food and having impeccable table manners." She laughed with a deep, mischievous chuckle. What I noticed from my time with Russell and Anne was that they shared about their lives very modestly, unaware of who they were *being* and the impact they have had on others. The qualities which were reflected in our conversations were his unswerving commitment to faith, commitment to developing young people, persistence, a strong marriage, valuing the input of others, humility, and a sense of humor.

Russell was born in 1919 and grew up in Ascot Vale with his parents and brother, Chris. Their mother was a Catholic; however, Russell didn't go to the Catholic school because there were eighty children in a class. His cousin Nancy went to that school and said it was a very poor standard. As a teenager, Russell was required to attend the Presbyterian church, as he played cricket with the team. He also enjoyed spending time at the stables at Flemington Racing

Club with a friend. He recalled that one Saturday night, they went dancing and had some rowdy fun.

He won a scholarship to University High School and attended until year ten. He joined the CMF (Citizens Military Forces) and did war service in New Guinea, being discharged in 1944. He came back to Melbourne on the train for the Victory March through Melbourne and then back to camp and a final posting at the Atherton Tablelands. After discharge, Russell went to the Melbourne Bible Institute (MBI) in November 1944 and spent two years studying theology. After MBI he went on to do Matriculation (AUSMAT) at Taylor's private college, which he had to also fund himself. His war service allowance had only funded his MBI studies.

He undertook his arts degree at Melbourne University, where he met Anne. After graduation he was invited to teach at Carey Grammar School in 1952. He spent thirty-three years at Carey influencing young people. The value in teaching them, and then playing football with them, really helped strengthen relationships.

Anne Costello (née Northrop) was born in 1929 and lived until 2022. One of four children, she was educated at St Michael's and obtained an arts degree from Melbourne University. As a child, she contracted rheumatic fever and was regarded as "delicate." She married Russell in 1953 but because of her impaired heart condition was discouraged from having children. Fortunately, she decided otherwise. She worked in teaching and as a psychologist and was actively involved with Russell and her family at Blackburn Baptist Church, which evolved into Crossways Baptist Church.

Even after Anne and Russell moved to Blackburn, my dad used to come up from North Balwyn to Main Street and pick them up, take them back for lunch, and then drive them home. When our cousin June married, I was their flower girl, and Julie, my sister, was upset. "I want to be a flower girl too," she sobbed. Anne and Russell offered to have Julie as their flower girl when they got married in 1953. Julie and I taught Tim, their son, to walk on holidays in Seaford, and he did so at ten months, which Anne said she regretted. Too active too early!

Apart from Anne's foundational Christian faith, her motivation to give back was fueled by her early illness. Her rheumatic fever meant that much of her nineteenth and twentieth years were spent in hospital, and even her wedding was delayed through her illness. When her doctor was visiting her in hospital, he advised her not to have children. As soon as he left the room she said to the nurse, "Fiddlesticks, what would he know!" Even during her pregnancy with Tim, the doctor suggested she abort the pregnancy. Fortunately, she didn't take his advice. Despite a weakened heart, she produced three healthy children, and this whole experience gave her a sense of urgency, not wanting to waste time but also to give back. Another aspect of her motivation was self-improvement. She was curious and interested to learn and valued the "furniture of the mind." She was always well-informed and articulate and contributed greatly to those students with whom she taught or counseled.

Russell became a committed Christian in late teens through his association with the local Presbyterian church. After leaving school, Russell worked in a textile factory, Dominion, making silk stockings, and he said it changed his life. Empire Towel factory, next door, gave Russell a job when he could no longer work at Dominion. During the Depression, jobs were difficult to find, so he was very appreciative. Chris, his brother, went to Footscray Tech and then worked in a bookshop.

Russell and Anne's children have all accomplished a great deal. Anne shared a photo taken in Canberra, when Peter was awarded a Companion Order of Australia (AC).[1] Peter took his

1. Peter Costello is Russell and Anne's second child, educated at Carey Grammar and attended Monash University, graduating in law. He was a member of the Federal House of Representatives from 1990 to 2009, deputy leader of the Liberals from 1994 to 2007, and involved with the International Monetary Fund as a governor of the World Bank and Asian Development Bank and as chairman of the G20 Central Bankers and Finance Ministers group. After leaving Parliament he served as a member and then chairman of the Independent Advisory Board of the World Bank in Washington (2009–2014). Peter published his memoirs in 2008 and was awarded the Companion Order of Australia (AC) in 2011. At the time of writing in 2023, he was chairman of the Australian Future Fund and chair of the Nine Entertainment Corporation.

son Sebastian and mother, Anne. Peter was a member of Federal Parliament for nineteen years and the longest serving treasurer in Australia's history. He now chairs the government's Future Fund. Tim[2] had already been awarded the Order of Australia, for his work in social advocacy and justice, and served as CEO for thirteen years and then as Advocate to World Vision until his departure in 2019. Janet[3] was the chaplain for Kilvington Grammar, a Baptist girls' school in Melbourne, and subsequently moved to Strathcona as their chaplain in 2021.

Russell passed away on May 24, 2016, at ninety-seven years old. The family arranged a service to celebrate his life at Crossway Baptist Church, and hundreds of people attended. Tim officiated, and both Peter and Janet spoke. Peter used the letters in his name to underscore several of Russell's qualities.

R — He was resilient

U — A unifier

S — A wonderful storyteller

S — A simple man with great humility

E — A lifelong educator

L — He was very loyal

L — He shared his love with so many

2. Tim Costello was appointed CEO to World Vision Australia in 2003 and worked tirelessly in the role until May 2016, when he stepped aside to become their Chief Advocate until June 2019. He moved on, citing the physical and emotional toll of the role over many years. He has since become the director of the Ethical Voice, executive director of Micah Australia, and a senior fellow at the Centre for Public Christianity. He has written eight books including *Streets of Hope: Finding God in St Kilda*, *Tips from a Travelling Soul-Searcher*, and *The Cost of Compassion*.

3. Janet Costello. Janet was educated at Strathcona Baptist Girls Grammar and went on to complete a bachelor of arts working as a teacher and student welfare coordinator before going on to complete her master of theology and graduate diploma in counseling. She was appointed chaplain at Kilvington Grammar School in 2012 and moved to the same role at Strathcona Girls School in 2021.

Peter said, "I don't think there was a man that I admired more than Russell. He was wise, humble, and showed love and mercy. He walked with God. He saw good in people, and even facing challenges would say, 'This too will pass.'" Peter remembered the tough love but also his sense of humor. He shared, "Russell loved his football and enjoyed the trips to Windy Hill to see Essendon play."

The Torch: Carey Community News ran a full-page obituary to Russell, documenting his school career of thirty-three years and his involvement in teaching sport and history.

It said, "Russell will always be held in high regard by the staff and students whose lives he touched." The obituary finished with an excerpt from "Farewell to My First Hero, My Father" by Tim Costello, his son, which Tim shared in the service. Russell was "a natural figure of authority and learning in his formative years but was also a source of great love, nurturing and wisdom." Death of a loved parent is always devastating. However, death is also a time of faith and for reflection, and he finished by saying, "I have taken great comfort in knowing that I have lived my father's lessons."[4]

Russell made a difference in my life because of the quality of his faith. He lived it every day. On the wall opposite the front door of their home was a special framed quote: "Christ is the head of this house. The unseen guest at every meal, the silent listener to every conversation."

Anne, as a teacher and psychologist, influenced me to do social work so I could contribute to others and impact social justice.

One never knows the ripple effect of who we are being and how it can impact on others.

TIM COSTELLO

August 5, 2013

I visited Tim in his World Vision office in Burwood after speaking with his executive assistant. I spoke with her about writing a book

---

4. Birrell et al., "Russell Costello."

on "making a difference" and my respect and admiration for Tim. I had already interviewed his father, Russell Costello, and mother, Anne Costello.

They are a special family indeed. I have also read several of Tim's books, including *Hope* and *Faith: Embracing Life in All Its Uncertainty*, and have used material from these books to elaborate on several of his responses.

What is the essence of Tim Costello? What shapes who you are?

In answer to this question, Tim spoke of sin and salvation, loving God and loving your neighbor. This is a universal commitment. According to Tim, Greco-Roman culture was very self-focused, in contrast to the Christian philosophy of giving to others.

Tim's Christian faith is a lived experience. "It has nourished the foundations of my life, making me who I am. It is a deep, broad, inclusive faith with a message of hope and reconciliation for our time." He has been touched, changed, and given purpose by his faith. Happiness is not the goal but a by-product of a deeper sense of purpose. Spirituality is about the relationship and connection with something bigger—something transcendent. For Tim, without a spiritual connection to God, "I struggle to find a deeper connection to who I am, to my neighbor, to the stranger in the world around me." Tim's inclusiveness means that he counts among his friends Buddhists, Hindus, and Muslims.

According to Tim, the American writer, scholar, and theologian David Bentley Hart comes closest to articulating Tim's experience of the divine, giving three reasons to believe: *being* or *existence, consciousness,* and *joy.*[5]

1. *Being* or *Existence.* Bentley Hart is reported to have said, "To see the cosmos as wholly pervaded, unified, and sustained by a divine intellectual power [is] at once transcendent and immanent."[6] This is what John's Gospel names as the *Logos,* who was with God and is God, and about whom Saint Paul

5. Hart, *Beauty of the Infinite.*

6. Hart, *Experience of God,* 59. David Bentley Hart is an American writer, philosopher, and religious studies scholar. He has written nineteen books and over a thousand shorter published pieces.

said, "In him we live and move and have our being" (Acts 17:28). Tim is "imbued with a sense of love and purpose in a sacred cosmos" and is inspired by a transfigured natural world full of beauty, love, and wonder. The question of why the solar system exists points him to a supreme being, the source of existence.

2. *Consciousness.* Tim says, "In my spiritual encounter, I had a change of consciousness and viewed the world differently. A supreme being and supreme mind gives rise to transparency of the universe, being open to consciousness and being comprehensible." Tim is fascinated by cultures, beliefs, and people.

3. *Joy.* There is a surge of joy and exuberance in Tim's life. He has an intuition of a transcendent sense of beauty. Longing for truth, for an understanding of reality, grants Tim purpose and a desire to see the profound interconnectedness in the world. Tim said, "Art at its heart [has] offered perspective on why my work and the world's poor is less about 'doing' and more about 'being' with them in solidarity, friendship, and inexplicable joy despite the poverty and suffering. My faith gives me joy and love as it hungers." Tim cited C. S. Lewis who wrote, "Joy is the serious business of heaven."[7]

Tim continued, "God is benevolence; therefore, as a vulnerable God, he entered our world and embraced our suffering and humanity. I see God in the face of Jesus. Salvation aims at understanding and wholeness. To be whole is to live with my faith, even if it puts me at risk of suffering and scorn. Spirituality as compared with philosophy is more about the choice to trust. Faith must be experienced and lived, and is embedded in my daily rhythm, and it is communal."

You have worked in several communities from St Kilda to Collins Street, Melbourne, and now World Vision. What has drawn you to this global organization?

World Vision Australia is a Christian relief development and advocacy organization, formed in the USA in 1950 with a focus

7. Lewis, *Letters to Malcolm*, 92–93.

on compassion, justice, and human rights.[8] WVA "works with children and families to overcome poverty and injustice," seeking to transform lives by tackling systemic causes of poverty.[9] World Vision works in countries around the world, including India, Africa, Indonesia, New Guinea, Vietnam, Cambodia, and East Timor. It also provides programs in Australian Aboriginal communities such as the Linking Hands program, working with young children. As well as responding to natural disasters they encourage child sponsorship to create a personal link between the giver and recipient, support workers in a range of countries, and encourage private partnerships in developmental programs.[10]

Tim is proud of the fact that World Vision has the biggest footprint in the Islamic world. Growing up in Blackburn, a very stable middle-class Caucasian suburb, he later moved to St Kilda, which offered a melting pot of cultures, social problems, and dysfunction. This was a radical shift. He learned his ethics locally in St Kilda and was able to translate them internationally.

Tim spoke of charity beginning and ending at home, and his concern about this perspective is that dignity is missing in certain approaches to charity. He is far more interested in empowerment. Tim is a teacher by profession, and that vocation is about asking questions to awaken others.

Frederick Buechner, an American Christian writer, spoke about calling intersecting with the world needs when he described vocation as the place where "your deep gladness and the world's deep hunger meet."[11] This quote beautifully describes Tim's mission.

---

8. World Vision is a global Christian aid agency that has been operating for over seventy years globally and in Australia since 1996. It is a Christian organization working with children, families, and communities to overcome poverty and injustice. WVA's vision is "for every child, life in all its fullness." At the time of writing, WVA was running 327 projects in forty countries. World Vision Australia, "About Us."

9. See World Vision Australia, "About Us."

10. See World Vision Australia, *2024 Annual Report*, "Program Sectors."

11. Buechner, *Wishful Thinking*, 95. Buechner was an American theologian who wrote about the Christian faith. To learn more about him, see www.frederickbuechner.com.

What shapes or motivates your commitment? How much do results impact your commitment?

One of the areas of strong commitment with significant results has been the fight against gambling.[12] Tim explains that one learns far more from being involved in these social justice issues and sees the importance of resilience. Tim is the Chief Advocate of the Alliance for Gambling Reform in Australia—an organization that works to prevent and minimize the harms caused by gambling.

Tim's life's work, as it has unfolded, has been about how faith addresses both the personal and impersonal, small and large, spiritual and social challenges, how it gives nourishment for private struggles but addresses public battles for justice. "It is so important to me," he said, "that my faith addresses violence, racism, poverty, and particularly our current issues of climate change and the world's sixty million refugees." Hence, he spends energy defending Australia's Overseas Development Assistance as it funds our national response to the global effort on impacting hunger and supporting refugees.[13] Tim is keen to see Australia's overseas aid contribution expand to 7–8 percent of the GDP.

William Carey, after whom Tim's school (Carey Baptist Grammar) was named, is another inspiration for Tim. Carey, born

12. Alliance for Gambling Reform is a national advocacy organization which works to prevent and minimize harm from gambling. Tim is their Chief Advocate and also a member of the Australian Churches Gambling Task Force. According to the Australian Institute of Health and Welfare, in 2022–2023, "total gambling expenditure (net losses) in Australia was $31.5 billion, the highest it has been in the last 2 decades." Between May 2022–April 2023, "$238.63 million was spent on gambling advertising on free-to-air TV, metro radio and online (including social media)." Australian Institute of Health and Welfare, "Gambling"; Australian Communications and Media Authority, "Gambling Advertising."

13. In 2023–2024, Australia donated approximately $4.77 billion in foreign aid, an increase on the 2021–2022 figure. The Department of Foreign Aid and Trade reports that the government is "committed to continued sustainable growth in Australia's ODA over the longer term. From 2026–27, we have locked in year-on-year ODA growth of 2.5 per cent per annum." Department of Foreign Affairs and Trade, "Development Assistance Budget." The OECD reports that in 2024, Australia's foreign aid spending represented 0.19 percent of its gross national income. OECD, "Development Co-Operation Profiles."

in 1761 in Northamptonshire, England, founded the English Baptist Missionary Society in 1792 and spent his life as a missionary in India. He translated the Bible into six Indo-Aryan languages and "parts of it into 29 other languages and dialects."[14] Carey founded and funded the establishment of Serampore College, an inclusive university that was the first in Asia with the power to grant Western-style university degrees.[15]

Tim cites Carey's famous maxim: "Expect great things from God; attempt great things for God."[16] "If we are all God's children, let us share a greater vision that includes the poor," Tim demands. He emphasizes that a hand up is preferable to a handout and that the contemporary modern focus on individual ownership leads to gross economic inequality. He champions fairness and works from the core assumption that "there should be no poor among us." Thus, the ethical challenge brought to the foreground in his work has been, "Will I make space for others, and at what cost or what personal sacrifice?" Yet this is more than a question of ethics; it is a question of being.

If God makes space for other beings, then we must do the same, explains Tim. Others' dignity must be deeply respected even if it offends our own prejudices, even if doing so is inconvenient or difficult.

What qualities have contributed to your success?

Tim believes that having a long-range vision, which has arisen from his faith, has been core to his success. This alongside a sense of calling and a commitment to outcomes—which also requires the patience to wait because achieving outcomes takes time and does not always occur. Tim spoke about "energy zones" and being able to sustain energy levels until a goal is achieved.

Tim cites the thirteenth-century Persian poet and Sufi mystic Jalal al-Din Rumi, who speaks of meeting in a field beyond wrongdoing and rightdoing.[17]

14. *Encyclopedia Britannica*, "William Carey," para. 1.

15. Serampore Municipality, "Sir William Carey."

16. Smith, *Life of William Carey*, 37.

17. See Rumi, *Essential Rumi*, 36. Jalal al-Din Muhammad Rumi

Tim affirms, "My faith says God is inviting us to that field. It is this larger faith dimension, and the questions it raises about all areas of life, be they personal, political, communal, or global, that drives me." He continues, "Faith opens the possibilities to speak of these mysteries, these imponderables: the universe, self, and other." When it comes to spiritual beliefs, Tim says he is "committed at the core, but open at the edges." He is committed to the way of Jesus, but Jesus' way was open to those in Palestine who were unclean and despised because Jesus taught that God loves them. He brought the outsiders in.

For Tim, humility is also important. He has developed a public profile but feels it is accidental. Tim observes that life is not linear; it is a surprising gift—so, humility is foundational. In speaking about humility, Tim says, "We need to be self-critical about the blindness of our superior insights. They may be just as real and no different to the same concepts of past generations we deplore."

When I ask Tim what legacy he'd like to leave, he says, "To encourage others to be fearless and courageous." World poverty has reduced in recent decades, and the Millenium Development Goals have committed to one billion people being out of poverty by 2030.[18] Similarly, the number of children dying from malnutrition and preventable diseases has significantly fallen over the last three decades.[19] But still, in 2023, *an estimated 13,100 children aged under five died each day from causes that are largely preventable, including undernutrition and disease.*[20] Tim feels that this number "in a world of plenty" is obscene.

(1207–1273) was a thirteenth-century Persian poet and Islamic scholar. Rumi's work has been lauded for expressing peace and tolerance and awareness through love. His poem, a rubai (four-line poem), is found in Divan-I Kebir.

18. According to the World Bank, "In 2025, an estimated 831 million people were living in extreme poverty, trying to live on less than $3 a day." World Bank, "Poverty." This figure increases to 1.1 billion when measured according to the holistic Multidimensional Poverty Index. See United Nations Development Programme, "Multi-Dimensional Poverty."

19. UNICEF, "Under-Five Mortality."

20. UNICEF, "Under-Five Mortality."

Tim brings the plight of the most vulnerable into our homes, our churches, our towns, and our halls of power—and we are convinced to lend a hand, to engage and share our resources. He invites us into a conversation where we discover a world in need of restoration and where we are inspired to be part of the solution. His faith engages with the real world and is not an escape: it involves joy and sorrow, blessing and burden. His faith envisions a society where all have a place at the table, no matter where we are born or which social strata we belong to.

"We are all under one law and one creator," says Tim. "Everyone is made in the image of God and of equal worth. Human rights are universal and indivisible because injustice to anyone, anywhere, is an injustice done to me. We are interconnected and we are family." Hope is a dominant thread, part of the tapestry of Tim's life over the past twenty years. "The symphony of anyone's life can have loud and calamitous parts," he reflects. "It takes discernment, patience, and deep listening to hear the soothing refrain of hope return."

Hope provides moments of inspiration in a challenging world. Tim cites Joan D. Chittister:

> Hope is what sits by a window and waits for one more
> dawn, despite the fact that there isn't one ounce of proof
> in tonight's black, black sky that it can possibly come.[21]

I am inspired by Tim because even though he has been motivated by Christian values, he has a way of straddling both the religious and secular worlds. His humility, authenticity, and willingness to take a stand despite opposition is most inspiring, and he has won a great deal of community respect. He shares many stories as a way of impacting others and making sense of our experiences. He is a masterful storyteller.

He has also resisted the political path which has allowed him the freedom to support the issues he believes in, without the

---

21. Chittister, *Scarred by Struggle*, 110. Chittister says, "It is the value of struggle that grows us" (43). Struggle builds the resilience required to endure the demands and challenges of life's journey.

challenge of party-political compromise. His motivation is very clear and authentic, and through his work and "who he is *being*," Tim really makes a difference in the world.

DUNCAN BROWN

May 5, 2013

Duncan was senior pastor at New Peninsula Baptist Church in Mount Martha, Victoria, from 2010 to 2015. It is a large progressive church with over six hundred people attending each week. Duncan is a very charismatic leader: as soon as I heard him speak, I was drawn to New Peninsula and felt a strong connection and resonance with the community. He is a wonderful communicator and had a series of high-profile people within his large network, including John Anderson, the former National party politician, and Greg Hunt, the former Liberal party member for Flinders, both of whom spoke at church during his tenure.

When I asked Duncan what his motivation was, he spoke about a calling to leadership and pastoring. Everyone is called and is required to live a life worthy of that calling, he explained. It may be an assignment for a season or a lifelong call, and it is important to be comfortable with the limitations and opportunities of the calling. He said, "My identity is who I am in Christ. His plan is already mapped out. The Spirit discerns how I use my gifts." He continued, "I have had a lifelong passion to mobilize people. Trained as a journalist, I worked for the not-for-profit sector with the Scripture Union in Queensland. Then I established a Christian consultancy which worked in the not-for-profit sector as well."

He shared about his partnership with Trish, his wife. Even though they are very different, she has enabled him to double the ministry capacity through her work, as well, with families and young children. They have discerned a rhythm on how they hear from God.

And hearing from God is something for everyone, according to Duncan. "God has shifted the cultural platform where people can discern their own direction," he explained. "Even though the New Peninsula Church leadership is with twenty-two elders, leadership is widespread through the church community. We are not compartmentalizing God: everyone has access to him."

Duncan recently took time off and led a group of drovers who managed a huge number of cattle traveling over hundreds of kilometers through North Queensland to find better pasture. What was his motivation to do that? His commitment is to mobilize people so they have the capacity to do amazing things. He sees the good in people. He indicated that Jim Collins's book[22] had made an impact on him and his style of leadership, particularly humility and fierce resolve.

LYDIA HARB

August 7, 2013

Lydia was the New Peninsula Community Caring Inc. CEO for several years from 2012 to 2015.[23] When I interviewed Lydia, she was heading up CCI Community Caring, a social justice outreach organization running several community programs on behalf of New Peninsula Baptist Church that included COACH Community Mentoring, Youth COACH, the Back on Track program (including food pantry), and the CCI Opportunity Shop with a community hub. The COACH program was created by Belinda Cowie and a group of NP staff and volunteers, and the program has now been implemented by many churches across Australia. It was developed to provide support for families under stress, and volunteers within the church community were trained to work with individuals to help them overcome life challenges. The program spread across the Peninsula and eventually nationally, and sponsorship moved to Crossway Church Burwood in 2020.

22. See Collins, *Good to Great*.

23. Community Caring Inc. was a separate entity to New Peninsula Baptist Church until 2023, when the structure was changed to incorporate it into New Peninsula Baptist Church (New Peninsula Caring).

Fundraising has been part of Lydia's management role, necessary to ensure the services could be maintained and expanded. I was interested to learn what motivated her to do what she did, as she seemed to go above and beyond what was required and spoke about her work with great passion. She had moved from the corporate environment, and her own training and HR consultancy, to the CCI CEO role and found it challenging to adapt to the different context and pace.

Lydia's focus was on empowerment, adding value and utilizing her skills to glorify God. The work of CCI involves helping people to see their potential. Within the community, the poor and vulnerable are hidden. CCI provides infrastructure services, and the programs are geared to mobilizing Christians, as volunteers, to contribute to making a positive and significant difference in the lives of these people in the local community. Lydia spoke about "a hand up rather than a handout." All the CCI clients are treated with respect, love, and dignity, and the volunteers are trained to work closely with the clients in both the COACH and Back on Track programs, empowering and supporting them in their lives and giving them the opportunity to grow and sustain their progress.

Together with a volunteer fundraising committee, Lydia and the team held several successful major COACH fundraising events from 2009 to 2013. Australian singer and entertainer Debra Byrne was the main performer at the 2013 gala at Lindenderry Winery at Red Hill, and as a Christian who held the COACH cause close to her heart, she was inspiring. Greg Hunt, the then–local federal member for Flinders, was a great supporter of COACH and donated auction items to support fundraising.

I asked her how she was able to accomplish that success.

"I handed it over to God. 'Be still and know that I am God' [Ps 46:10]. Be prepared to wait for his timing."

The work of CCI is about breaking generational poverty and working with young families, reaching out and partnering with them, encouraging them to know that they can achieve whatever they set their minds to. CCI staff see their job as a vocation, and this creates a very committed culture.

Having women in leadership positions is not supported by all Christian communities.

However, Duncan Brown, senior pastor at New Peninsula Church during Lydia's time as CCI CEO, was very pro–female leadership. He supported the appointment of female pastors to the eldership and encouraged Lydia to take up the role of CCI CEO. When asked to take on the role, Lydia didn't see herself as a social justice advocate, nor an expert in the area. What she did have, however, was compassion. She was inspired by the Bible verse, "I have anointed you to preach the good news to the poor" (Isa 61:1, Luke 4:18).

Lydia focused on action rather than words. She met with the board members, staff, volunteers, and clients to develop strong relationships and an understanding of what they wanted CCI to achieve.

In 2015, the COACH program had expanded to the point where coordinating a national program was beyond the scope of New Peninsula's remit. At that time Mission Australia, under the leadership of Toby Hall, was keen to take over the running of the national COACH program. Lydia then moved into the role of Mission Australia COACH's general manager. After twelve months and a change of CEO, Mission Australia decided COACH was not aligned to their vision for the future, and so a few other sponsors were canvassed. Ultimately Crossway Church took on the role of running the national program with Mark Matthews managing the national roll out.

Lydia's work had been vital for the development and growth of the program—and other Community Caring Inc. ventures—making a difference in the lives of many individuals and families across Australia.

KATHERINE BARLING

May 4, 2013

I met Katherine through the personal development work I did through Landmark Worldwide (previously known as Landmark

Education), a transformational ontological program that enables people to grasp their humanity and live a life of possibility.[24] Katherine and I began a conversation about "making a difference" and the arenas in which we choose to do so. I had focused on the wider community and global arenas; however, she turned my ideas on their head. She found working in her local community and within community action groups easy, but her challenge was to commit to spending time with her autistic nephew, Will, who had been left without a carer or family support.

I was keen to interview her to explore what her motivation and underlying values were in making the decision to support her nephew. What were the factors that shaped her life towards contribution?

Katherine shared with me, "I was faced with a set of circumstances. My brother Craig couldn't take care of his sixteen-year-old son, Will's mother had died the previous year, and I was the most appropriate family member to step in." Katherine continued, "I saw it as the right thing to do. It was forwarding life for everyone."

After discussion with her brother Craig, Will's father, and understanding that he wanted this solution, she made the commitment to have Will live with her. "I also made a learning commitment" she added. "I wanted to develop Will, to strengthen his relationships and the quality of his interactions and have him function as independently as possible."

Katherine wouldn't have thought she'd be that sort of sister or aunt to take on primary caring duties. However, once she saw what was going on and what was needed, she was willing to act. She moved back into the family home and gave up her full-time work to look after Will.

After Will had been with her a few months, Katherine opened the door for Will to think about his future. "I took on an education role, teaching Will to find his own way, in very small steps," Katherine shared. "Will would stay in his own world. He had different wiring, so would make different assumptions, and there would be sensory differences."

24. See their website at landmarkworldwide.com.

Katherine began teaching and guiding Will, not knowing if it would be successful. She put herself in Will's world, doing things like taking him shopping to buy food wherever he wanted to go. She helped Will understand how to operate the public transport card (Myki) and get credit to it.

She was affirming in assuring him that he could manage such tasks on his own. She used everyday experiences as learning opportunities and had the expectation that he could learn to think and act for himself. Katherine has been there to answer Will's questions. They have fun together. On one occasion they were "tourists" in Melbourne.

In her community work, Katherine's commitment had been generosity and giving to others, with an inclusive attitude. When it came to caring for Will, she felt a degree of being overwhelmed. She has a lot of respect for carers, especially as they are often not being heard within the wider community. Her motivation has come from a commitment to empower Will and help him develop to his full potential, and stand by him as he develops his independence. She put his needs ahead of her own in making this decision.

The value and the joy for Katherine have been knowing that Will sees his own future now and can make it happen.

Within the family context, there was a lack of acknowledgment for Katherine's contribution. She also felt compassion for Will's siblings. Having an autistic brother often meant that their needs came second, and there was a level of resentment towards him. Will felt that they should be more confident and optimistic about his future.

While Will was living with Katherine, his father passed away. At his father's funeral, Will's response was to go up and ask people attending how they knew his father. Auntie Kath stood with him when he spoke. "I felt this showed significant courage on Will's part," she confided.

Will has made considerable progress. Sometimes he brings in Kath's washing. Sometimes he gives her a hug when he's happy. She hopes that he can develop "meta cognition"—the ability to think about what is going on—and self-reflection.

After caring for Will for twelve months, Katherine enquired about community facilities where he could move to strengthen his independence. She felt he was ready for this next stage, and she would maintain regular contact. He was excited yet apprehensive. The step has worked well. He can communicate his needs and feels very proud to share his progress with Katherine. He enjoys going back to their place to have a meal together. Katherine is looking to go back to community development work now that Will is settled in his independent supported accommodation.

JEAN-PAUL SAMPUTU

March 2018

I was put in contact with Jean-Paul through an American friend whom I met locally who had worked with Jean-Paul in New York, when he was performing, and was inspired by his story.

Jean-Paul is a remarkable Rwandan man who was alive during the Rwandan genocide in 1994, when up to a million people were killed as extremist Hutu leaders exploited divisions entrenched during the colonial era to justify the mass murder of Tutsis and moderate Hutus.[25]

As Tutsis, Jean-Paul's parents, three brothers, and sister were murdered by a childhood Christian friend, Vincent, a Hutu. Jean-Paul went through nine very dark years until through his faith, and dialogue with God, he chose forgiveness.

---

25. In speaking of the 1994 Rwandan genocide, the United Nations reports that around one million people died and around 250,000 women were raped. Of course, this left "the country's population traumatized and its infrastructure decimated." However, Rwanda has since "embarked on an ambitious justice and reconciliation process" to pursue peace. Since 1994, "more than 120,000 people were detained and accused of . . . criminal responsibility" for their part in the genocide. "To deal with [this] number of perpetrators, a judicial response was pursued on three levels: the International Criminal Tribunal for Rwanda, the national court system, and the Gacaca courts." United Nations, *Justice and Reconciliation*, 1.

His purpose is to share his powerful message of *love, forgiveness,* and *reconciliation* through songs and telling his story: to bring like-minded community and Christian groups together with a call to action and the skills needed to create a new paradigm.

"The conflict and disharmony and questionable values of the world at present makes the need for the Christian message of love, forgiveness, and reconciliation even more critical," he shared. Jean-Paul challenges us to reflect on the current culture of revenge. Is this the legacy we want to leave for our children? Do we have the courage to forgive? Can we create a new paradigm for people to live by?

In 2003, nine years after the genocide trauma, Jean-Paul did not believe in God. He was almost dying from excessive drinking, had no peace, and was burning with anger, bitterness, and resentment. People were praying for him to recover and for healing. Then Jean-Paul had a remarkable set of experiences.

> During a prayer, I heard a voice. It was telling me, "You can't kill yourself. You didn't create yourself, so you don't have the right to take your life, and besides, it is not time yet. You need to repel the bandage of bitterness and resentment and embrace forgiveness." I woke up and was amazed at the experience, but others who were present didn't hear the voice.
>
> I went to the witch doctors to help me. They confessed that they couldn't solve my problems, only God can solve them. "You have chosen Satan, but God has the power. We are agents of the enemy," they said. I prayed again but was blocked by the genocide. I didn't want to forget it. I wrote a song called "Where Were You?" which became very popular with the Rwandans, challenging God [for] allow[ing] such atrocities to occur. Where was he when my family and community were slaughtered?
>
> Later (in 2003), I went to Prayer Mountain in Uganda. It is a mountain that is used for meditation. I wanted to find God myself, not through pastors and churches but spending three months alone with God. I studied Genesis—"In the beginning . . ."—and some questions formed in my mind.

Jean-Paul asked God, "Why did you create me?"

> God seemed to be telling me it was to show love. "How can I in such extenuating circumstances?" I said to him. The Hutus killed because they didn't follow the gospel. Moses brought down the commandments, and the laws dictated that you love your neighbor as yourself and that you love God. But genocide? Love means praying for your enemies.
>
> "Love bears all things, believes all things, hopes all things, and endures all things" [1 Cor 13:7]. That gave me room in my heart for love, and I learnt who a Christian really was. I resisted, and then finally agreed; I am ready to forgive.
>
> As a singer, everything changed. I changed my music and praised God in all my songs. As a singer and songwriter, I tour the world with this powerful message of love, forgiveness, and reconciliation.
>
> In 2004, I went back to Butari, the village where I was born, to a traditional gathering "Gacaca."[26] I met Vincent, one of the perpetrators of my family's genocide, and used restorative justice from our ancestors. I spoke publicly and shared that God had told me to forgive. We had known each other from childhood. We were both very happy I forgave him publicly, and we embraced.

What Jean-Paul hadn't expected was the reaction from some of the villagers present. They were critical and angry and were questioning his motivation. What did he want? "There were journalists and cameramen. I was interviewed. I felt very happy, even victorious. Vincent took me to where my father had been buried, and we started the process of reconciliation. We have remained close friends, and I was invited by Vincent's wife to attend his funeral in Rwanda in 2019."

---

26. "In the Gacaca system, communities at the local level elected judges to hear the trials of [accused] genocide suspects," though this did not include those who were accused of being part of the planning of the genocide (they had to appear before the national court). "The courts gave lower sentences if the person was repentant and sought reconciliation with the community." United Nations, *Justice and Reconciliation*, 2.

Jean-Paul challenges us with the question, "What communities do you want to impact?"

> The message of forgiveness is relevant for everyone, everywhere, all around the world. We don't teach this in universities but need to give this message in schools. Jesus said [that] people [would] recognize his disciples. . . . It's about forgiveness and love.
>
> We have created a culture of revenge. Bin Laden was killed, but in doing so we created many more Bin Ladens. How can we create peace? We can't change the past but can learn from it. We are responsible for the culture that is created for our children. Education rather than violence. Politics needs to change. We don't know the opposite of killing. We need to be willing to change, to consider the heritage for our children. We continue to create the mistakes of our ancestors. We need to create a "culture of forgiveness." Our conditioning shapes the attitudes of our children. We need to take on being great ancestors so our message is one of love and reconciliation.

Ingela, Jean-Paul's musical group, was created to share his music several years before the genocide. When traveling, he can invite others to join the Ingela performance, spread his message, and inspire celebration and dancing.

Jean-Paul provided a wonderful concert and workshop at New Peninsula Church, sharing his message. When Jean-Paul was acknowledged in the session for his courage in forgiving Vincent, he indicated that it was God working through him; Jean-Paul didn't ever take the credit.

People left feeling very inspired and moved and were encouraged to explore three questions in their own lives:

- Who do I need to forgive?

- Who do I need to ask forgiveness of?

- What do I need to forgive myself for?

Above all, Jean-Paul's message is about love and reconciliation, and his Christian beliefs have been a foundation for his ongoing commitment to these values.

HELEN MACNAUGHTAN

September 2018

Helen was a nurse and missionary in Papua New Guinea for thirty-three years.

I agreed to meet Helen Macnaughtan at the Pier café in Frankston, overlooking Port Phillip Bay. She had piqued my interest by sharing that she had spent over three decades working in Papua New Guinea. I was keen to understand what motivated her to leave New Zealand and then Australia and spend so much of her life serving others.

Helen grew up in New Zealand.

> I was born in 1939, the eldest of five children, and my father left the family when I was eleven years old. My mother was a Christian, but my father did not have a faith. I belonged to a Crusader group at school and in my teens spent a week at a Youth for Christ camp and was encouraged in my Christian faith. I was also influenced by Paul Smith, the son of Oswald J. Smith from the People's Church in Toronto, Canada, who visited Palmerston North in New Zealand in 1956. At one of his rallies, I offered myself to the Lord.

Helen undertook nursing training and went on to study midwifery in Wellington before attending the Bible college in Auckland.

"I felt a strong call to missionary work," she explained. "Despite three proposals of marriage, I decided to go to Papua New Guinea as a single person, content that I knew where God had sent me."

In 1965, Helen moved to the Papua New Guinea Highlands. She was quite isolated, but the senior missionaries were very supportive. While in the lowlands at a field conference, she met Ken

Macnaughtan. He had gone to Papua New Guinea in 1963 as a missionary as well.

"Ken continued to write to me," she shared.

> He proposed, and we married in September 1967. I was working at Orokana [a village in the Southern Highlands of Papua New Guinea], while Ken had been stationed at Samberigi [another village in the Southern Highlands approximately twenty-five miles from Orokana]. We were married in Samberigi and spent a further three months there, before returning to Australia for eight months furlough (now called home assignment). Our wedding was a simple affair. I planted food for the wedding breakfast, and the mission field planes were the taxis to bring in our guests. My mother brought the simple wedding dress from Australia.

When Helen and Ken each went initially to PNG, the mission organization supported them financially. Subsequently, however, a different system was introduced called Team Support, which meant that they were required to raise their own funds to support their work. This became their role back in Australia, where they initially lived with Ken's parents.

After eight months' furlough, in late 1968 they returned to PNG. In 1969, their first child, Ian, was born, followed by Andrea in 1972 and Rachel in 1974. Helen homeschooled the children while working as a nurse, training two local midwives and dispensary staff. The family was based ten miles from the government hospital and had to travel on very rough roads to get there. Helen taught health and hygiene at the maternal and child welfare clinics, as well as birth control, including the whole cycle of fertilization to the actual delivery of a baby. The local people had many misconceptions! Helen and Ken improved nutrition by introducing more diverse foods to villagers (whose diet had been previously constituted by sago, fish, bush rats, and spiders) and by encouraging men to help in the garden. Where sago was the staple food, producing crops was more than a full-time job for the women.

Papua New Guinea has over eight hundred languages and numerous dialects. Helen and Ken translated and taught the Scriptures in their local communities.

> Traditionally the local people were an animistic people who believed that the spirits lived in trees, rocks, stones, rivers, and so on. They didn't worship the spirits; they feared them and needed to appease them in different ways. When the gospel came with the truth of Jesus who brought freedom from fear, and the promise of forgiveness and eternal life, their lives were changed radically. Especially for the women—who traditionally were put on the same level as pigs—it was life changing. The women came to know that they were loved and accepted equally by God; they were no longer inferior. By grounding the local people in the Scriptures, this gave them a foundation to build their lives on, and to guard against false teaching and heresy.

Based in Samberigi, Ken translated the New Testament into the Huli language, and Helen did the proofreading and editing. Helen continued,

> Ken and I also ran marriage enrichment seminars in different areas, mainly for church leaders, and that was also very enlightening and enriching. Couples could only come if both husband and wife attended, as Ken and I wanted to guard against one or the other going home and telling their partner where they needed to improve! They really enjoyed those sessions. For some of the time, they met as a whole group; for others, Ken took the men and I took the women for matters particularly pertinent for them.
>
> During our last six years, we were based in Mendi. We worked with church leaders and pastors, discipling them and grounding them in the Scriptures, often communicating in Pidgin English.
>
> We had a rewarding experience in Papua New Guinea and believe we positively impacted those we worked with.

JULIE PARKE

May 7, 2018

I was interested to meet with Julie as I knew that she and her husband, Peter, have been fostering children since the early nineties. Julie and Peter, who have now been married for twenty-eight years, weren't able to have any children of their own. Peter had been married previously and had three children, one of whom has Down's syndrome. Peter and Julie explored adoption and IVF, but these options weren't successful. Her maternal instincts kicked in, and she was really struggling to cope when she couldn't meet this nurturing need.

Julie spoke with Dale Stevenson, then–senior pastor at their church, New Peninsula, and shared her God-given desire for motherhood. She asked for prayer, and Dale prayed with Julie. She shared with me that a warmth flowed through her, and she knew that whatever happened, she would be fine. She learned to rely on God.

Julie had begun to work in the disability field with a family support service provided through Oz Child, a leading Australian child-welfare organization. Through that role, Julie formed a special bond with a young client named Jasmine.

"After a few years," explains Julie,

> I learnt that Jasmine could be up for long-term fostering. So, Peter and I began the process. The challenge was that Jasmine needed a high level of care. She had an intellectual disability, couldn't speak, needed feeding and nappies. However, after several years of assessment, Peter and I began fostering Jasmine when she was thirteen years old.

She continued,

> Even though we realized that caring for her was going to be very challenging, I knew that Jasmine was just right for us. She has special school during the day and was with us in the evenings.
>
> Jasmine stayed with Peter and I for six years, until she was eighteen years old. We were keen to keep her for

longer, but at eighteen years, many of the support services were terminated, and so we reluctantly placed her in supported accommodation. We continued to see her weekly and have her home in the holidays.

Following Jasmine's departure, Julie and Peter continued to provide respite for other families. Dala was a baby they took at a very young age. She had serious medical issues, and Julie stayed at Monash Medical Centre for five weeks undergoing training to care for her. Dala had to be PEG-fed and was allowed home from the hospital to Julie and Peter at thirteen months of age.

Julie and Peter cared for Dala for six months, with her father having scheduled access to her. Dala returned to live with her mother after six months.

Another infant, Tom, was only three days old when Julie and Peter took him in. They cared for him for twenty months. Then, Julie and Peter applied for permanent fostering but were told that they were too old. At the same time, they were caring for Tony for over eighteen months, who had behavioral issues.

Although Julie and Peter are not fostering at present, they do have ongoing contact with several of the children for whom they cared.

The respite they offer is sometimes emergency care, so they could be called at three o'clock in the morning to take in a child.

The experience has been very satisfying for Julie and Peter, and they have made a difference in the lives of many children and families They feel it has all been part of God's plan.

CAS (CAROLYN) TAYLOR

April 11, 2018

I met with Cas Taylor at the New Peninsula Community Caring Opportunity Shop where she was manager from 2013 until 2023. The "Opp Shop" is a large store in the Australian seaside town of Mornington. It sells a range of pre-loved furniture, clothing, toys, and bric-a-brac. The store is open six days a week. Cas manages between fifty and fifty-six volunteers, six of whom have a team leader role with the volunteers that they are scheduled with each week.

The volunteers are attracted from a range of sources. A significant number are local church members. Cas also works in conjunction with the Australian government's Work for the Dole scheme to place people who need work experience. There are between fifteen and twenty-five people from this group over the course of a year, and more than twelve gain paid employment because of their experience. Cas also has several people who have disabilities and who benefit from personal interaction and work experience. In this way the shop has a social enterprise role.

The volunteers have a range of roles in the Opportunity Shop. Apart from team leaders, volunteers are trained as cashiers, front-of-store people, and visual merchandisers, or in sorting and pricing in the back area. Others assist with the photographing for online sales, documenting and management, and pickup and delivery with their van. As well as selling goods though the Opportunity Shop, Cas has also successfully sold a considerable number of high-value goods online, ensuring higher returns for sought-after items.

What motivates Cas to undertake such a challenging role? Her vision is sharing love—in fact expressing Jesus' love. She has created a caring community where people feel accepted and included. For the work experience volunteers, she is keen for them to learn, to have a positive experience, and feel valued. Customers feel welcome, and a number come in every week and so have formed relationships with the volunteers. Some customers stay for coffee in the kitchen area, so there is a sense that the shop is developing as a community hub. Cas has a way of making everyone feel special. The Opportunity Shop generates funding for Community Caring outreach services that New Peninsula Church provides.

Cas works long hours as not only is she running a large enterprise, but she also must manage the rostering of volunteers, the online program, and sorting and values assessments of new donations.

I have been involved with the Opp Shop in the delivery of a few customer engagement and communication training sessions, and I get a real sense that the volunteers love coming to serve, and they do feel valued and an important part of the team.

JAMIE EDGERTON

September 15, 2022

Jamie is a remarkable man. I met with him to discuss what motivated him in his life's work. I am struck by his humility but also his lifelong quest for spiritual growth with practical applications in his journey to follow Jesus. This was a central motivation for all that he has accomplished.

Jamie's is a very holistic faith encompassing addressing world poverty, social justice, the environment, and First Nations self-determination. He conjures up a picture of a spoked wheel, with Jesus at the center as the integrating force and the spokes reaching out and influencing all these important areas of life.

His guiding text: "He has shown you, O man, what is good; and what does the Lord require of you but to do justice, and to love kindness, and to walk humbly with your God" (Mic 6:8).[27]

Jamie's early influences were St. Hilary's Anglican Church in Kew, Rev. Peter Corney at the St. Hilary's Youth Club, and Carey Baptist Grammar School, which he attended from early primary level. The chaplain of Carey, Rev. Alan Wright, had a huge influence on Jamie's faith journey, both during Jamie's secondary school years and for many subsequent decades. Alan's approach to teaching religious education was unconventional: rather than focusing solely on Scripture, he led students to examine the realities of life in neighboring communities, and globally, and then helped them reflect on these in the light of Scripture. On one occasion in a senior class, Alan showed a documentary on the then-current famine in Rajasthan and the response of the UN Food for Work

27. "Micah was an early prophet. His messages concerning Samaria and Jerusalem are a clarion call to repentance and righteousness." Clow, *Bible Reader's Encyclopaedia*, 250.

program.[28] Jamie was haunted by the images of landless and illiterate peasants carrying headloads of soil up a steep slope in scorching temperatures, only to be compensated with enough rice to keep their families alive. The product of their toil was a dam and an irrigation system for the landed upper class, further entrenching existing inequalities.

Other Carey secondary teachers had an important influence on Jamie's political leanings. His English teacher, Llew Evans, encouraged Jamie to review Eleanor Dark's classic historical novel about the First Fleet and early settlement years, *The Timeless Land*.[29] The book's sensitive and prescient depiction of the impact of the invasion on the local Indigenous communities played a formative role in Jamie's lifelong passion for First Nations justice. Another English teacher, John Sykes, was the adviser to the school's inter-school debating team, which Jamie led. A host school that year, Jamie's team had the choice of which side to adopt on a proposition that Australia should support the US during the Vietnam War. John advised the team to argue against the current national policy, on the grounds that it would be easier to win the debate. Jamie's extensive research on the issue led not only to a resounding victory in the debate but to a strong tendency to distrust the prevalent knee-jerk conservative views in his family and church circles.

By the end of secondary school, Jamie was strongly motivated to devote his career to making an impact on the lives of people experiencing hunger and poverty. Accordingly, he enrolled in the Agricultural Science course at Melbourne University. During the long vacation after his second year of study, Jamie took advantage of an Australian university students' package to spend twelve weeks visiting community development projects and ashrams in India and Nepal. This experience had a significant impact on him, and after his return, he joined and then led the university's

---

28. Under the UN Food for Work program, the Indian government provided work for poor people related to the construction of basic unpaved roads, clearing debris, etc. and gave food grains instead of wages. See the website for the UN World Food Programme at https://www.wfp.org.

29. Dark, *Timeless Land*.

Community Aid Abroad (CAA) club. Over the course of the next few years, Jamie served on the state, and later the national, committee of CAA.[30]

In the early seventies, Jamie (now married to his lifelong love, Julie) was enrolled in a PhD program. But he had a sense that his career was heading in a wrong direction. When the leader of a CAA-supported educational institute at Kosbad Hill in India visited Melbourne, Jamie was inspired to explore the possibility of a volunteer assignment. Months later, Jamie asked Julie if she would agree to him truncating his post-graduate studies (with a master's degree) and embarking on an adventure to work in India for two years.

Despite the disbelief and anxieties of their parents, and with the financial support of a local CAA group, Jamie and Julie set off to live and work with the same CAA-supported institute located at Kosbad Hill, about 160 km north of Bombay (now Mumbai). Jamie had two roles, working in both pasture plant introduction and the training of local Indigenous students. Julie, a trained nurse and midwife, started clinical outreach services in the hamlets around the village, after discovering the dearth of medical services in their locale. Towards the end of their stay, the World Bank recruited Jamie through their Young Professionals Program, which focused on recruiting individuals with a passion for international development.[31]

Jamie worked with the World Bank in Washington, DC, for eight years within the Rural Development Division. This was a newly formed unit with the mandate of working in the poorest countries to address the needs of small farmers, who were perceived to be central to addressing world poverty. Here, Jamie was confronted by the failure of the established system to focus on

---

30. The Oxfam Australia website states that CAA "began in Melbourne in 1953 as a church-affiliated group called Food for Peace Campaign, founded by Father Gerard Kennedy Tucker. . . . In 1962, a full-time campaign director was appointed and the name changed to Community Aid Abroad [CAA]." CAA was a founding member of Oxfam International, at which point its name was "changed to Oxfam Community Aid Abroad in 2001 and then to Oxfam Australia in 2005." Oxfam Australia, "About Us."

31. See World Bank Group, "WBG Young Professionals Program."

landless laborers, who are the poorest and most disenfranchised group in society. To explore this issue, Jamie took two years leave without pay to work with the Christian advocacy organization Bread for the World (BFW), located close to the US Congress.[32] He led a small team to develop study materials for the BFW citizen advocacy groups across the USA and a corresponding legislative initiative on the issue of "Land and Hunger." But Jamie became quite disillusioned with the corruption and unregulated election funding on Capitol Hill.

For most of the eight-year period in Washington, DC, Julie and Jamie worshiped with the Sojourners Community—a pacifist Christian community of activists led by Rev. Jim Wallis.[33] They lived in a group household and were involved with Sojourners' local ministries in a poor, black, inner-city neighborhood. They participated in frequent nonviolent protests against apartheid in South Africa and the arms race.

Early in the 1980s Jamie retired from the World Bank and returned to Australia. Julie and Jamie (now with two young children) settled in Cairns in tropical North Queensland. Julie drew on her nursing skills to work with an Indigenous-led Mother and Children Centre just outside Cairns, and Jamie established a consultancy company, Tropical Research Management, to undertake poverty-focused international assignments, as well as providing Aboriginal development services in Cape York and the Northern Territory. Jamie also volunteered with a team led by a senior Aboriginal lawman,

32. "Bread for the World is a USA-based Christian advocacy organization urging government decision makers to do all they can to pursue a world without hunger. Their mission is to educate and equip people to advocate for policies and programs that can help end hunger in the US and around the world." Bread for the World, "About Us."

33. Sojourners is an ecumenical Christian media and advocacy organization focused on social and racial justice. It was started as an activist Christian community in the early 1970s by a group of students from the Trinity Evangelical Divinity School in Chicago, including the Christian writer and leader Rev. Jim Wallis. The community moved to Washington, DC, in 1975. It disbanded as an intentional community toward the end of the 1990s, but continues to publish its award-winning magazine, *Sojourners*. See Sojourners, "History of Sojourners."

Pastor George Rosendale, under the auspices of a Darwin-based ecumenical adult education agency, Nungalinya College.[34]

The team provided community development training for Aboriginal Christian leaders in several Cape York communities.

After nearly a decade living in Cairns, Jamie was recruited back to the World Bank to train World Bank staff and member country officials with the Economic Development Institute (EDI).[35] His role as a senior participation specialist provided numerous opportunities to pilot participatory approaches to development. He introduced a field-based workshop approach to enable poor communities in Sierra Leone to influence the design of the government's Poverty Reduction Strategy Paper. In collaboration with like-minded World Bank colleagues and international non-governmental organizations, Jamie elaborated and piloted an approach to empower marginalized and mostly illiterate community members to hold local government education and health services accountable. The approach increased the awareness of participants of their rights to decent services; the deficiencies in their own local services; and the opportunities to address these deficiencies through local collective action. This came to be known as Community Based Performance Monitoring (CBPM).[36]

Jamie's work on CBPM became known to World Vision Australia (WVA). He was engaged to work with a WVA team led by

34. Nungalinya is a Darwin-based Combined Churches Training College for Indigenous Australians. It provides training for Christian ministers and community leadership. See their website at https://www.nungalinya.edu.au.

35. The World Bank Economic Development Institute (EDI) is now called the World Bank Institute. The institute's objective is to be "an initiative for global collaboration in tackling key development challenges." It brings together "think tanks, academics, and experts," especially aiming to amplify voices from developing countries. World Bank Group, "Our Work."

36. This process involves drawing in, activating, motivating, and empowering the community and its representatives to give feedback directly about the functioning of local public services such as primary health centers and primary schools. In the World Vision context, it evolved into Citizen Voice and Action (CVA) and is now operating in over fifty countries being implemented in hundreds of development programs. World Vision International, *Citizen Voice and Action.*

Bill Walker and World Vision staff in Uganda and Brazil to introduce the CBPM approach to ongoing World Vision activities. The pilot programs were very successful, and in due course, WVA developed an expanded and mainstreamed version of CBPM named Citizen Voice and Action (CVA). CVA has now been used in over fifty countries and is impacting thousands of marginalized communities.

WVA's CBPM/CVA process was underpinned by a team of disciplined people engaged in intercessory prayer. This team was comprised of two of Jamie's teachers (by then retired): Rev. Alan Wright and Llew Evans. Their prayers were informed by regular updates on progress and challenges provided by Jamie and Bill Walker. The interactive process between Jamie as an Aid and Development Practitioner, and Alan and Bill as part of an actively praying community—continued over about ten years—was an exhilarating one. It has been described by Alan, Jamie, and Bill in several reflective papers published by World Vision International, drawing on the notion of "Engaged Spirituality" as described in Janet W. Parachin's 1999 book of the same name.[37] Jamie described the experience as "practicing discipleship on the wings of prayer and providence."

After a total of ten years in Washington, DC, Jamie retired from the World Bank for a second time. He returned to Australia and settled on the Mornington Peninsula with most of his family (their oldest son chose to stay in the US to forge a career in information technology and later started his own family). Jamie continued professional work as an international consultant for many years. He and Julie became very active in co-establishing three outreach ministries within the New Peninsula Baptist Church: Jigsaw, a missional community in a local disadvantaged area;[38] support for a

---

37. See Wright et al., *Engaged Spirituality*; Parachin, *Engaged Spirituality*.

38. The Jigsaw missional community has been ministering in east Mornington, Victoria, since the early 2000s. In addition to providing a weekly meal and fellowship in a local community center, Jigsaw operates two outreach services: the Home Ground Café, offering training for disadvantaged youth, and a Community House. It is run independently from New Peninsula Church.

Christian Indigenous mission in the Pilbara, Western Australia;[39] and a thriving partnership between New Peninsula Church and a church in northeast Uganda.[40]

Over the course of his journey, Jamie has been able to seize some great opportunities, while working through numerous obstacles. Now retired from professional work, his central motivation to serve the Lord hasn't wavered. Jamie and Julie remain members of the Jigsaw missional community and are founding members of the Devilbend Foundation Inc., established to support the restoration and management of the nearby Devilbend Natural Features Reserve. Jamie continues links with First Nations leaders and communities. He and Julie are also active in a local performative branch of the Extinction Rebellion climate action movement[41] and are actively involved with Liquid Church, in the seaside town of Mount Martha.

39. The Indigenous Partnership Group (IPG) operated from 2010–2021 as an outreach of New Peninsula Baptist Church (NP) on the Mornington Peninsula in Victoria. IPG provided financial and on-site support to two missionaries (John and Angela Wilmot) ministering to Indigenous residents of Newman in the Pilbara region of Western Australia. The Wilmots continue their ministry as an independent agency, Red Dirt Blue Sky, providing holistic support to the Martu people of the Western Desert.

40. The Uganda Partnership Group (UPG) commenced in the mid-2000s as an outreach of New Peninsula Baptist Church (NP) on the Mornington Peninsula in Victoria. It has evolved into an active partnership between NP and Bethel Baptist Church in Mbale, Uganda. In addition to providing financial support for Bethel Church's planting of and support for twelve satellite churches in the predominantly animist and Muslim communities in the surrounding area, UPG organizes annual exchange visits between the two churches (alternating between visits by Bethel leaders to Australia, and exposure visits by NP members to Uganda).

41. Extinction Rebellion is a UK-founded global environmental movement that uses nonviolent civil disobedience to demand government action on climate change. See their website at https://rebellion.global.

INDIVIDUAL FACTORS WHICH FUELED THE DIFFERENCE MAKERS' MOTIVATION

Russell's Motivation

Russell's context for motivation was his Christian belief. Over many years, he contributed to generations of students at Carey Grammar but also shared his skills and knowledge in his Bible college work. In terms of his impact, his consistent and long-term career commitment provided great value. He also significantly influenced his sons, Tim and Peter, and daughter, Janet. Peter was treasurer from 1996–2007 in the Australian Federal Government during the Howard era and was a member of the House of Representatives from 1990–2009. Russell and Anne's daughter, Janet, an ordained minister, was chaplain at the Kilvington Baptist school for several years and in 2020 became chaplain at Strathcona Girls Grammar School in Canterbury.

Anne's Motivation

Anne, too, was motivated by her Christian faith, and she, too, chose a career of teaching and psychology with a commitment to contribute to others and see them grow and develop. Her impact as a role model on her family was profound. Anne was also motivated by her early illness and her sense of urgency in making the most of her life.

Tim's Motivation

Tim's motivational context was his Christian commitment to service, alongside the use of his gifts to contribute to others. However, there was also anger and indignation at the injustice in the world. He asks the question, If we are all God's children why is there such inequality, poverty, and exploitation? His values and ethics railed at the seduction and lure of gambling, the huge financial and emotional cost to families, and the government's investment through taxation gains. But more than that, he had the courage to act and challenge the accepted views and attitudes, often at huge personal cost.

Duncan's Motivation

Duncan indicated that his calling was to leadership and pastoring. He spoke about "spirit-led" gifting—the Spirit discerning how he used his gifts. He spoke about a lifelong passion to mobilize people to do amazing things. Duncan is motivated by seeing the good in people. And in his work in the not-for-profit sector, Duncan, too, was motivated by righteous anger and holy discontent.

Lydia's Motivation

Lydia was motivated by her Christian commitment and the opportunity that Duncan opened for her, believing in her ability to take on a leadership role. She was able to utilize her organizational and corporate skills to manage CCI along with her gifting with networking and fundraising.

Katherine's Motivation

Katherine was faced with a family situation of need and saw that she was the best person to provide support for her nephew. In choosing to take this opportunity she had to give up her existing career. She was motivated by seeing the growth opportunity for Will and being able to share her communication and insight skills to develop Will's adaptability, flexibility, and life skills. She had a commitment to contributing to the greater good and making the world a better place.

Jean-Paul's Motivation

Jean-Paul faced ten years of obstacles before his motivation spurred him into action. He was consumed by anger at the genocide of his family, which he turned in on himself, and it was only when he reached a low point in his life that he turned to God and listened to the concern of his friends. He saw, through his interaction with God, the power of forgiveness and the courage needed to let go of his anger and resentment. This not only led to restoring his relationship with Vincent, the perpetrator, but opening his heart to sharing his story and tapping into his musical gifts.

Helen's Motivation

Helen was initially motivated by her Christian values to contribute to others, particularly those in countries which were undeveloped, like Papua New Guinea. She wanted to share her nursing skills and pass on nutritional knowledge to the village women. She used the message of God's love to raise the status of women in the village and impact their own attitudes of subservience and low value, and to improve the quality of their relationships. She and Ken also put their language and biblical knowledge into translating the Bible into Huli, a native language, so the village people's lives could be guided by the Bible's wisdom.

Julie's Motivation

Julie was motivated by her Christian values of contribution but also recognized her own needs to care for children, when she was unable to have her own. She and Peter opened their home to children with disabilities who were often vulnerable and shared their love with these foster children, who had often been rejected by their own families. Frequently the children's behavior was challenging, stressful, and difficult to manage. Despite these obstacles, Julie and Peter provided this service over several decades, to a range of different children.

Cas's Motivation

Cas's primary motivation was expressing and sharing Jesus' love, creating a valuable and caring community full of acceptance, taking into account the individual differences of volunteers and work-experience team members. She was also motivated to share her skills in managing others and in aspects of the shop organization, sharing her entrepreneurial skills through online sales of high-value donations and generating significant funds for NPCCI.

Jamie's Motivation

Jamie's motivation arose from his Christian faith and flowed from a sense of responsibility to the world in addressing issues of inequality, poverty, and environmental sustainability. He seized several opportunities and showed courage in trusting that everything would work out as intended. His commitment to take action was very wide-ranging and holistic and has continued since being back in Australia.

COMMON THEMES WHICH EMERGED FROM THE INTERVIEWS WITH THE DIFFERENCE MAKERS

- *Spiritual Values.* A majority of those interviewed were motivated by their Christian values in their commitment to contribute to others. Christ set an example of showing love, acceptance, forgiveness, and inclusion, which provides a role model for most of the eleven interviewees.

- *Being Passionate About Issues.* This often seems to flow from having a Christian faith as well as lived experience of social issues. Tim's passion for social justice has influenced his actions, Jean-Paul's passion was for forgiveness, Cas's for creating a nurturing and empowering social enterprise community, and Helen's passion was for empowering the PNG community through her interest in health, equality, and her translating of the Gospels into the local language.

- *Anger and Indignation.* Tim's anger played a key role in fueling his motivation. His righteous indignation over poverty has led to his global contribution as CEO and Advocate for World Vision for fifteen years, and now heading up the Micah Challenge, and sharing his ideas and insights through a significant number of publications and speaking engagements. His anger at the high penetration of gambling accessibility and addiction in Australia, especially in lower socioeconomic areas, has led to him forming a coalition against gambling and being a regular spokesperson on the matter in the media. Jean-Paul's anger has enabled a commensurate depth of forgiveness, and his motivation to share this gift of love has been sustained for almost twenty years.

- *Role Models and Mentors.* Role models and mentors were also key in motivating several of the people interviewed. Tim was very influenced by both his parents and the Swiss theologian Torwald Lorenzen during his international theology course. Jamie was influenced by several of his Carey teachers and the youth worker from St Hilary's. Duncan was a very powerful mentor for Lydia, inspiring her to take on the CCI responsibility, and Helen spoke of the role Youth for Christ members and Paul Smith from the People's Church, Toronto played in her formative years.

- *Sharing Their Skills.* Identifying their particular skills and using those in their contribution to others was key for each of the interviewees. Katherine's skills included personal development experience, insight, and communication; Helen's were her nursing and relationship skills; and Jamie's were sharing his agricultural skills in his early work in India, but also his organizational and empowerment capabilities in his work with the World Bank and his CBPM contribution. Julie shared her gifts of caring, empathy, and acceptance. Lydia has great networking and fundraising skills, and Duncan and Tim are very charismatic and are inspirational speakers and communicators. Russell was a committed educator who shared his love of history and sport with students, and his biblical knowledge with Bible college attendees. Anne, too, was a committed educator and psychologist, and Jean-Paul has used his music and communication skills to share his story with many others.

- *Facing a Crisis or Personal Challenge*. Jean-Paul not only had to cope with the trauma of losing five members of his family in the Rwandan genocide, but with his anger and bitterness that pervaded his life for the next ten years. His friends intervened, and after a message from God, he was able to forgive the perpetrator and share his story through song. Julie, too, was unable to have children or adopt and so decided to foster children who had disabilities to give them a loving and supportive home. Katherine faced the challenge of her autistic nephew losing his mother and his father not able to cope with him, so she gave up her job to care for him in his key formative years.

- *Seizing Opportunities*. Several people interviewed were proactive is seizing opportunities rather than letting them pass by. Tim moved from local ministry to his role at World Vision; Lydia moved from corporate training into the Community Caring leadership; and Cas took on the management of the NP Opportunity Shop when it was facing a few challenges. Julie was proactive in looking outwards for a "contribution" solution rather than focusing on what was missing in her life. Jamie, too, seized several opportunities that came his way, showing both courage and persistence.

- *Demonstrating Leadership*. A number of those people interviewed were motivated to empower others and show leadership in harnessing others' energy and commitment. Russell, Tim, Jean-Paul, Lydia, Helen, and Jamie demonstrate this most clearly.

- *Issues Addressed.* The people interviewed addressed a range of issues through their commitments. Russell and Anne's were education and faith; Tim's was social justice, poverty eradication, addressing gambling accessibility and addiction, inclusion, acceptance, and faith; Duncan's focus was raising awareness of faith and developing people's potential; Lydia's was on empowering the disadvantaged; Jean-Paul's commitment was raising awareness and fostering forgiveness and reconciliation; Helen's contribution had a very practical focus through health and well-being education and trusting relationships and sharing her faith, while Katherine's contribution was about empowerment, relationships, and education; Julie provided opportunities and caring for marginalized and disadvantaged children; Cas's was empowerment, relationships, and sharing her faith; and Jamie made a difference through education, tackling social justice, and empowerment through Citizen Voice and Action, with engaged spirituality and environmental care.

Photos of the Eleven
Difference Makers

Russell Costello
Photo provided by Tim Costello. Reproduced with his permission.

Anne Costello
Photo provided by Tim Costello. Reproduced with his permission.

Tim Costello
Photo provided by Tim Costello. Reproduced with his permission.

Duncan Brown
Photo provided by Duncan Brown. Reproduced with his permission.

Lydia Harb
Photo provided by Lydia Harb. Reproduced with her permission.

Katherine Barling
Photo provided by Katherine Barling. Reproduced with her permission.

Jean-Paul Samputu
Photo provided by Jean-Paul Samputu. Reproduced with his permission.

Helen Macnaughtan
Photo provided by Helen Macnaughtan. Reproduced with her permission.

Julie Parke
Photo provided by Julie Parke. Reproduced with her permission.

Cas (Carolyn) Taylor
Photo provided by Cas Taylor. Reproduced with her permission.

Jamie Edgerton
Photo provided by Jamie Edgerton. Reproduced with his permission.

3

Exploring Pathways to Action

WHAT IS THE PROCESS OF
MAKING A DIFFERENCE?

NOW THAT WE HAVE explored some fascinating people who have made a difference in their particular spheres, we can reflect on the process that they have undertaken to do so.

The foundation seems to be knowing and understanding yourself, recognizing your strengths, skills, and areas you need to develop. From this foundation, it is important to explore what "lights you up" and fires up your passion. Most of the group were motivated by Christian values and so were looking at how they could contribute to others by following Christ's example. It seems that having spiritual beliefs that guide your behavior can create that bigger context for action. The next step is to develop a vision and goals, identifying the strategy and time frame for planning and action.

It's also an opportunity to think about the legacy you would like to leave for others—what do you want to take action on and why?

Most people who set a big goal face obstacles and challenges on the journey. Having the ability to work through these issues and stay focused on the vision is paramount.

A further step can be enrolling others in your vision: demonstrating leadership and creating community to build momentum.

OVERCOMING OBSTACLES: CREATING URGENCY, PERSISTENCE, AND SUSTAINABILITY

Eckhart Tolle in *The Power of Now* asks a series of questions. What I glean from his writing is that life is only lived in the present moment: "The timeless state of intense conscious presence in the Now."[1] We often hanker after the past or dream for the future, but focusing on the "now" gives us a sense of urgency. Time and life are precious, and the time to act is now.

Each of the interviewees has faced significant obstacles—I think particularly of Jean-Paul, Julie, and Jamie—but they persisted and overcame them. The obstacles they faced were a mixture of external and internal barriers.

Obstacles and roadblocks can be anticipated with most projects, but how we handle them is key. Do we let them derail or discourage us, or solve them to move forward? Ensuring sustainability of our project or goal could mean asking a mentor for support, engaging others in our project, or passing the baton to others to ensure succession and the project's ongoing viability. One of the factors that often can impede our progress towards achieving a goal to make a difference is procrastination. Often it may be related to fear of failure, uncertainty, or not knowing where to start, but it results in putting off action. To overcome procrastination, we can strengthen the quality of persistence.

Albert Schweitzer, theologian and missionary doctor, is often credited as having said, "The real tragedy of man is what dies inside him whilst he still lives." While the quotation isn't contained in any of his writings, it does capture the spirit of his thought. Let's

---

1. Tolle, *Power of Now*, 5.

explore what gets in the way of making a difference and how we can overcome some common barriers to action.

CREATING AN EMPOWERING MINDSET

Creating the right mindset in overcoming both internal and external barriers can be foundational—we must be clear that we *can* make a difference. This allows us to be persistent and not give up too easily.

Sometimes the idea of a project is so overwhelming we don't even start in the first place; we are apathetic or buy into the mindset that we can't make a difference. Approaching a project one step at a time, and trusting in the power of small steps, can help us to feel less overwhelmed by big goals.

Another barrier to action is lack of trust: questioning the validity of the organization that we may consider contributing to, or the proportion of funds used wisely. While it is essential to do our due diligence in assessing the integrity of the groups we might contribute to, fear can also inhibit our willingness to commit. Talking to others who are already involved can be another good way of gaining important insights and of developing the courage to commit. Often, the best way to overcome fear is to act.

Maybe judgmental attitudes impede our willingness to act too. *Why would I want to help them?* An unfortunately common and often misguided attitude is to blame others for their misfortune: *They are responsible for their own circumstances; why can't they help themselves?* But blaming others doesn't solve anything, and we rarely have all the information needed to make fair judgments of others' lives. Does blaming others actually *help* them to overcome their challenges? Does it make the world a better place? Or can we accept that life is complex, that suffering *happens*, and that we can be part of the solution?

So, an empowering mindset is one with a strong commitment to fulfillment; a willingness to overcome fear and roadblocks; an open, nonjudgmental mind; the courage to keep going; and the willingness to trust and engage with others to achieve a shared goal.

HARNESSING YOUR PASSION

We spoke earlier about being passionate about what we'd like to achieve. How do we tap into our passion so we can truly make a difference?

Ask yourself, Am I passionate about my life?

Henry Thoreau observed that "the mass of men lead lives of quiet desperation. What is called resignation is confirmed desperation."[2] Is this so? How do we avoid living a life of "quiet desperation"?

As previously explored, George Bernard Shaw perhaps offers part of the solution:

> This is the true joy of life, the being used for a purpose recognized by yourself as a mighty one; . . . the being a force of nature instead of a feverish, selfish little clod of ailments and grievances, complaining that the world will not devote itself to making you happy.[3]

Being passionate and being with people who are inspiring and passionate is very energizing and helps to create a bigger purpose and context for our lives.

So, what makes us passionate? What gives us energy and enthusiasm? It is an important question to ponder given that this is our real life and not a practice run.

Do we know what we are passionate about? The key is to think about what we love doing—whether we are paid for it or not. What gives us energy and enthusiasm? What is our authentic self-expression? Being passionate is about engaging in an activity that lifts our spirits and allows us to be at one with ourselves, lose track of time, and be fully absorbed. Sometimes it involves risk-taking, stepping outside what is comfortable and moving into the unknown.

It is also about doing things we feel we are good at, giving us a sense of accomplishment. It is often the challenge of taking things to the next level, so we stretch and grow.

2. Thoreau, *Walden*, 7.

3. Shaw, *Man and Superman*, xxxii ("To Arthur Bingham Walkley").

Thoreau also said, "If one advances confidently in the direction of his dreams and endeavours to live the life which he has imagined, he will meet with success unexpected in common hours."[4]

Some people's passion involves an individual pursuit: the tranquility of painting in the outback or writing in the solitude of your study. For others, it involves operating in a team; partnership with others and camaraderie gives a feeling of exhilaration. Within a team, we can also be a participant or an observer: the football players and the supporters. Both groups have different roles but can be equally passionate.

Why is doing something you are passionate about important? Passion means we will be motivated to spend time investing in that area we care about; we will be able to sustain our commitment and overcome obstacles and have an unshakable determination to accomplish our goals. Our inspiration can then enroll others, enthuse our team, and compel us to action.

I have identified that what I love doing is contributing to others, and this has had a number of expressions:

- Developing people in their workplace: advancing their skills as managers and leaders

- Giving people access to personal development: growing in self-awareness, acceptance, and understanding

- Creating beautiful handcrafts for special people in my life

- Making a difference on the planet through a commitment to sustainability, world peace, and ending hunger

- Expressing my passions through writing: communicating with others

- Contributing to my family and communities

Some of these self-expressions are through my professional work; others I do because I love to do them—and I do them within the context of contributing and making a difference.

4. Thoreau, *Walden*, 250.

What I have seen from my personal developmental journey is that our internal view of what we do, our internal conversation, plays such a key role in our experience of life. I am reminded of the story of the stonemason who was working on a building with his team. A passerby asked the stonemason's apprentice, "What are you doing?"

"I am chipping stone," he said.

The person moved on to the next stonemason. "Tell me what you are doing?" he asked.

"I am building a wall," the next stonemason responded.

The observer moved to the next stonemason, working further along the building, and asked again, "What are you doing?"

The last stonemason stood up and said proudly, "I am building a cathedral."

So, what can we learn from this story for ourselves? Can we inject new passion into our job, our relationships, or areas of interest just by examining the way we view the context in which we operate? Maybe the people whom we look up to, who are very successful and accomplished at what they do, simply have an inspired way of seeing the context in which they operate. Do we take on giving this to others and help others to see the context of their contribution with passion and positivity, by giving them encouraging feedback, affirming their contribution, and reenforcing their participation?

For ourselves, keeping the passion alive takes courage. Passion can be sustained through affirmations, reading, being coached, spending time with like-minded people, and consciously creating an inspired context every day.

What are the benefits of passion?

You feel alive, inspired, and able to inspire others!

You have a sense of satisfaction and accomplishment in what you do, and there is an ease and lack of stress.

You will feel you have shared your song with others.

And what is the cost of *not* being passionate? Life will be mediocre. You will feel more like a leaf in the wind than a raging torrent and may look back with regret at missed opportunities. Your song will still be with you, unexpressed.

You have control over your life and your passions, and it is your choice how you move forward.

I am suggesting we think about these questions:

- If I were given a life to live, how would I live it?

- If I were given the opportunity to do something with 100 percent chance of success and with no chance of failure, what would I do?

As the poet Oliver Wendell Holmes Sr. wrote,

> Alas for those that never sing,
> But die with all their music in them![5]

So, connect with your passion, be at peace with yourself, and be an inspiration to others! The choice to do so is yours.

RIPPLES THAT IMPACT OTHERS: THE POWER OF LEADERSHIP

How do we inspire and shape ourselves and others to be bigger than we know ourselves to be, and enroll others in our vision?

Several of the people I interviewed used their leadership to engage and empower others in making a difference. I'm particularly thinking of Tim, Russell and Jean-Paul, Duncan, Lydia, and Helen. One can achieve a certain amount on one's own, but being able to enroll others in what we are committed to provides extraordinary leverage to make a profound difference. In exploring leadership over many years, the most empowering models that I have found have been set out in the following books:

- Joseph Jaworski's *Synchronicity: The Inner Path of Leadership*

---

5. Holmes, "Voiceless," stanza 1, lines 6–8.

- Robert Greenleaf's *Servant Leadership: A Journey into the Nature of Legitimate Power and Greatness*[6]

- Bernard Bass and Ronald E. Riggio's *Transformational Leadership: A Comprehensive Review of Theory and Research* and *Leadership and Performance Beyond Expectations*

Showing leadership is a key role in expanding and sharing your vision.

Synchronicity: The Inner Path of Leadership opens a very rich conversation about the essence of leadership. Jaworski sees it as "a commitment of being" and a "fundamental shift of mind."[7] He references *character, integrity, responsibility, relatedness, interconnectedness,* and *wholeness.* "New leadership must be grounded in fundamentally new understandings of how the world works" and "fundamentally new ways of thinking."[8] Jaworski encourages us to allow leadership to unfold through each of us.

Greenleaf sees servant leadership as based in who we are being, and our capacity to serve. "The philosophy [of servant leadership] focuses primarily on the growth and wellbeing of people and their communities." The servant leader "make[s] sure that other people's highest priority needs are being served."[9] The assumption is that everyone has leadership potential, which gives rise to a bigger question: What are we collectively able to create?

Bass and Riggio's notion of "transformational leadership" reflects strong commitment and broad visionary ideas; it is creative rather than reactionary leadership. Transformational leadership involves inspiring and motivating others by optimistically communicating a vision; fostering teamwork, and a culture of respect and encouragement; and being an admired role model. It also involves openness to new ideas, innovation, and creativity, particularly in relation to problem-solving and the embrace of mistakes

---

6. Greenleaf established the Center for Servant Leadership.

7. Senge, introduction to *Synchronicity*, 12, 11.

8. Senge, introduction to *Synchronicity*, 9. See also ch. 24, "Creating the Future" (esp. 183–85).

9. Greenleaf, *Servant as Leader*, 7.

as opportunities for growth. A great leader attends and listens to their team members' needs and shows respect, support, and empathy, while modeling open communication.[10]

Exploring the concept of leadership encourages us to consider the following questions:

- In what ways can my leadership empower the project I am working on?

- What model of leadership is the most appropriate to empower me and my team?

PATHWAYS TO MAKE A DIFFERENCE

Christian Values: Giving of Yourself

Most people interviewed were motivated by their Christian values.

Christ's life was one of contribution, and he invited his followers to do the same. He embraced the "outsiders"—those who were foreigners, sick, disabled, shunned by society—and healed them. He lived very simply and humbly.

So today, he challenges his followers in a very materialistic, conflict-ridden, and individually focused world to *love God and love our neighbor as ourselves*. A Christian's basic values that flow from love are acceptance, empathy, and contribution: these are powerful motivators for making a difference on this planet.

"This is my commandment, that you love one another as I have loved you. . . . This I command you, to love one another" (John 15:12, 17).

Time or Material Giving

Most of the people interviewed gave of themselves, their time, and personal resources when working for the causes they were passionate about. Former US President Bill Clinton explores a range

10. Bass and Riggio, *Transformational Leadership*.

of different ways of giving in his book titled *Giving*. We all can give, says Clinton, whether it be through money, time, resources, ideas and energy, Giving makes a difference. Through giving, we express our individual values and preferences and our communal interconnectedness.[11]

So how does "giving" relate to "making a difference"? Does all giving "make a difference"? If we explore the "charity" model, where there is an inequality between the giver and receiver, there is often a dependency created without empowering the receiver to be a solution-finder. Another "giving" dilemma we face is highlighted in the example of "the beggar on the street." Do we respond to him? And if so, how? Do we simply walk past, or give him money, food, or a card with information on the local homeless shelter? Do we sit down with him and really identify what is going on in his life and then try to help in other ways? Do we consider the short-term or longer-term implications of our actions? Do we look at the situation from our perspective or that of the recipient?

As mentioned, one organization that I have a strong commitment to is The Hunger Project. This organization is committed to ending hunger on the planet, and when it started the conversation on ending hunger in the 1970s, doing so was seen as impossible. The United Nations agreed upon the Millenium Development Goals in 2000 and instituted the Sustainable Development Goals in 2015 (Including "Goal 1: No Poverty" and "Goal 2: No Hunger"), and all the UN member states have agreed to these.[12] Of course, THP supports these goals.

Rather than seeing the hungry people of the world as a problem, The Hunger Project sees them as the *solution* to their own hunger. Through working alongside the local people and training them, local groups can be mobilized, becoming epicenters for medical and maternity care, microcredit, access to clean water, AIDS education, and literacy opportunities—and these are needs identified by communities themselves. The "charity" model is replaced by the "empowerment" model, with people taking control

11. Clinton, *Giving*.
12. United Nations, "17 Goals."

of their lives and solving their most urgent needs, as well as ensuring sustainability in the future. The Hunger Project's Vision, Commitment, and Action workshops have been used in many countries to "build and strengthen the social capital necessary for all sustainable change."[13]

Where is our hunger? The empowered people in developing countries often have very few material possessions but have an appreciation of the simple pleasures in life. Do we have a hunger of material possessions, continually acquiring more, bigger, faster, better? Do our possessions give us satisfaction, or do they actually increase our insatiability? Is our individualist hunger damaging our spirit of community and collaboration?

A New Moral Code

In Jim Wallis's extraordinary book *Seven Ways to Change the World*, Wallis contrasts the notion of a "career" with the idea of a *vocation* or *calling*. Vocation, teaches Wallis, comes from pursuing a connection between our "best talents and skills" and our "truest and deepest values."[14]

Wallis writes,

> Ask where your gifts intersect with the groaning needs of the world—right there is your vocation. The antidote to cynicism is not optimism but action, and action is finally born out of hope. It is about believing that the world can be changed, because it is only that belief that ever changes the world. And if not us, who will believe it? If not you, then who?[15]

Let us not forget Christ's words: "All things are possible to him who believes" (Mark 9:23).

The key is to ask who you really are and who you want to become. It is to ask what you believe you are supposed to do with

13. The Hunger Project, *Yes We Can*, 2.

14. Wallis, *Seven Ways*, 236.

15. Wallis, *Seven Ways*, 236.

your life. Consider your calling, your moral compass—then dare to dream things and don't be afraid to take risks.

Wallis also highlights the connection between spirituality and social justice.[16] "Being accountable to the facts of injustice and the need to change them," he writes, "is the only way for the spiritual life to have real authenticity. Without a commitment to justice, the search for spirituality can easily become self-serving."[17]

But Wallis points out that society will never change if change does not also occur in us personally—that is, "societal transformation" always comes with "personal transformation."[18] And faith plays a key role here, providing "the fire, the passion, the strength, the perseverance and the hope necessary for social movements to win and to change politics."[19]

When the going gets tough and even risky or dangerous, many people will give up—unless they have learned to tap into the deep resources of faith, in the way of Desmond Tutu and Nelson Mandela. Faith reminds us that change is always possible. Christians live the values of the "new order of the Kingdom of God," living as an "alternative community" to "engage the world around critical and specific issues of injustice, to hold the state accountable and limit its use of force, to always maintain a global perspective and to seek the common good of the place where we find ourselves."[20] This is a vital message in times such as these.

Working Together

Wallis emphasizes the importance of community for change-making. Rather than using the values of faith to divide people on certain moral issues, Wallis says that these values should function as " a bridge to unite us on the truly important issues in our public

16. Wallis, *Seven Ways*, 20.

17. Wallis, *Seven Ways*, 237.

18. Wallis, *Seven Ways*, 16.

19. Wallis, *Seven Ways*, 16.

20. Wallis, *Seven Ways*, 64.

life."[21] "Common good politics" should take the place of "the politics of individual gain and special interests."[22]

What is common good? The *Catechism of the Catholic Church* describes it as "the sum total of social conditions which allow people, either as groups or individuals, to reach their fulfillment more fully and more easily."[23] The African concept of *ubuntu* offers powerful insight into what it means to seek good for everyone. Archbishop Desmond Tutu describes *ubuntu* as "the essence of being human. We say a person is a person through other persons. We are made for togetherness."[24] Furthermore, "for ubuntu, the *summum bonum*, the greatest good is communal harmony. . . . If one person is dehumanized, then inexorably we are all diminished and dehumanized in our turn."[25]

The Center for American Progress explains that "the common good approach to politics represents a clear break with the radical individualism, corruption and greed that defines contemporary American life. It marks the end of a politics that leaves people to rise and fall on their own."[26]

Jim Wallis suggests three steps to "inclusion and justice."[27]

(1) Compassion for those who are suffering, which drives us to focus on the next step

(2) Social justice questions—"Why are things like this?"

(3) "A critical movement into solidarity, community or interdependence with the poor," which comes when we realize our "destinies [are] ultimately tied up with one another"[28]

---

21. Wallis, *Seven Ways*, 66.

22. Wallis, *Seven Ways*, 66.

23. *Catechism of the Catholic Church*, no. 1906, citing Vatican II, *Gaudium et Spes*, no. 26.

24. Tutu, "Longford Lecture," para. 13.

25. Tutu, "Longford Lecture," para. 14.

26. Center for American Progress, "Common Good Conference."

27. Wallis, *Seven Ways*, 98.

28. Wallis, *Seven Ways*, 99.

Tackling the Critical Issues

What are the key issues that we need to focus on in making change within our world today?

In my interviews with difference makers, the following themes emerged. There are of course, many more.

- Social injustice and exploitation of the poor by the rich

- Poverty and social exclusion

- Under-resourcing of families

- Gambling reduction and control

- Refugee acceptance and integration

- First Nations empowerment

- Climate justice

Based on the interviewees' insights and subsequent reflections, making a difference seems to be fostered and empowered by the following:

- Having a strong belief system and values, such as Christian commitment

- Finding an empowering context for action, such as working towards ending hunger, working in a developing country, enriching the lives of others

- Using your talents and gifts, skills and abilities

- Being concerned about social justice, poverty, inequality, or our environment

- Having a commitment to the greater good and wanting to make a difference

- Being willing to look beyond one's personal or family needs or gratification

- Having a sense and inner drive that you *can* make a difference on your own or through your faith

- Being passionate, with a desire to enroll others and help them catch the vision

- Having perseverance to overcome obstacles and keep focused

- Being willing to pay a personal cost in order to do something extraordinary

In this chapter, we have explored several pathways to action individually, but also communally. We have drilled down into being passionate and considered a few different leadership models, exploring how to empower others to become involved in our projects while also considering our own values and motivations. Many of the community issues we face currently are in urgent need of change, so our actions and commitment are critical to impacting them powerfully. The next step is to provide you with your own personal template, where you can begin working through the various steps and considerations, so you can be inspired and motivated to act in the area in which you want to make a difference.

4

How Can I Make a Difference?

HOW CAN I MAKE A DIFFERENCE?

I HAVE SPOKEN WITH a group of ordinary people who have shown an extraordinary commitment to others. Making a difference is about shifting focus from yourself to others. One needs to have a sense of self-worth to be able to move the focus from oneself to others. Making a difference also requires an empowering mind-set—we must really believe that we *can* make a difference. For the Christians I interviewed, making a difference also depended on putting themselves in the Lord's hands and being guided by him in the direction they took.

Taking the journey should be as important as the destination. This involves thinking about the process, as well as the outcomes.

CORE VALUES AND CONTEXT

What are the core values that shape your "making a difference"?

- Love of others, and for the Christians, sharing God's love

- Contribution: focusing on others

- Mutual respect and trust

- Putting other's needs before your own

- Seeing the bigger picture, and playing a big game

- Persistence, perseverance, and patience

- Collaboration: working with others who share our passion

- Taking responsibility for commitment and completion

Here are ten key steps to help you with the process and a template to follow so you can design your own tapestry of contribution.

KNOW YOUR PASSION:
TEN STEPS TO FULFILLMENT

How do you know what your passion is? Some people are very clear about their passion, but others struggle to identify it. Here are some steps to help you clarify what it is and how to go about fulfilling it:

1. Think about what you love to do. What gives you joy and fulfillment?

2. Spend some time thinking about your skills and attributes. You may have a skill with your hands, a creative pursuit, a sporting interest, or you may love being with people.

3. Identify your core values. What is important to you and forms the basis of your attitudes and behavior? In which contexts do you express your values? Our values and attitudes shape who we are "being."

4. What issues do you want to address? What challenges are you or your community facing at present, or what opportunities can you create? Spend time surfing the internet to crystallize your ideas and explore opportunities. Think about who you admire in a similar field. Does this provide an opening or idea for action? If money, time, and resources were unlimited, what would you want to do?

5. Creating a vision and goals. The ability to translate the vision into action requires consideration of time frames, resources, and a robust process of engagement.

6. Do you want to enroll others in your vision? Being able to transfer skills to others and empower them provides a pathway for sustainable outcomes. Is there a community or organization who shares your vision? Would a mentor be worthwhile for you for support and direction?

7. Review any obstacles that you might have. Is your mindset conducive to action, or is it stopping you? Can you work with other like-minded people to overcome these obstacles? Consider both internal and external obstacles and how they can be overcome.

8. Reflection and review. Is the project on track? How can we reshape it to align with our goals? Prayer and meditation are important for the Christian so that our thoughts and actions are guided by the Lord.

9. What are the benefits to achieving your goal? Who is going to benefit and how?

10. Celebrating your success and acknowledging each milestone. This is important—taking time to reflect on what has been achieved, and the effort that has been put in, is a critical part of any process.

You are welcome to make contact and share your progress via mattwood@bigpond.net.au

My Personal Action Plan

1. Identify my passion.

2. Clarify my core values.

3. Identify my strengths and skills.

4. What issues do I want to impact—locally, nationally, or globally?

5.   Develop a vision and goal, strategy, and time frames.

6.   Who do I want to enroll to share my vision?

7.   What is likely to get in the way? Identify obstacles and possible solutions.

8.   Reflection and review. Am I on track to achieve my goal?

9.   What are the benefits to achieving my goal?

10. Celebrating my success.

Appendix 1

Circles of Self-Expression
and Contribution

Appendix 2

Maslow's Hierarchy of Needs

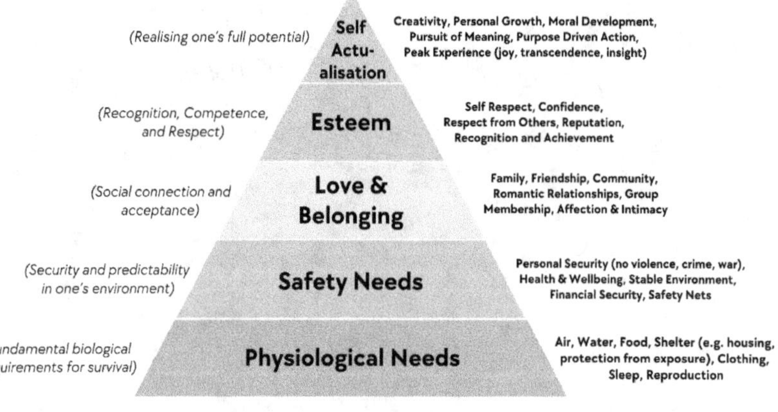

"Maslow's Hierarchy of Needs Diagram." Image by Hamish.coker. Wikimedia Commons. CC-BY-SA 4.0.

Bibliography

Australian Communications and Media Authority. "Gambling Advertising in Australia: Placement and Spending." Last updated Dec. 15, 2023. https://www.acma.gov.au/publications/2023-10/report/gambling-advertising-australia-placement-and-spending.

Australian Institute of Health and Welfare. "Gambling." Oct. 16, 2025. https://www.aihw.gov.au/reports/australias-welfare/gambling.

Baldwin, Elizabeth, and Kate Griffiths. "Big Gambling Is Playing with Our Democracy." Grattan Institute, Nov. 20, 2023. https://grattan.edu.au/news/big-gambling-is-playing-with-our-democracy/.

Bartley, William Warren, III. *Werner Erhard: The Transformation of a Man; The Founding of Est.* New York: Clarkson N. Potter, 1978.

Bass, Bernard M., and Ronald E. Riggio. *Transformational Leadership: A Comprehensive Review of Theory and Research and Leadership and Performance Beyond Expectations.* 2nd ed. New Jersey: Lawrence Erlbaum Associates, 2006.

Berne, Eric. *Games People Play: The Psychology of Human Relationships.* Middlesex: Penguin, 1964.

Bickersteth, Edward. *A Treatise on Prayer.* Philadelphia: Hooker & Agnew, 1841.

Birrell, Kate, et al. "Obituary: Russell Costello." *Torch: Carey Community News,* Summer 2016, 45. https://archives.carey.com.au/nodes/view/3182.

Bread for the World. "About Us." https://www.bread.org/about/.

Brown, Brené. *Daring Greatly.* London: Penguin, 2016.

Buechner, Frederick. *Wishful Thinking: A Theological ABC.* New York: Harper & Row, 1973.

Catechism of the Catholic Church. 2nd ed. Vatican City: Libreria Editrice Vaticana, 1997.

Center for American Progress. "Common Good Conference." Oct. 18, 2006. https://www.americanprogress.org/events/common-good-conference/.

Chittister, Joan D. *Scarred by Struggle, Transformed by Hope.* Grand Rapids: Eerdmans, 2003.

Clinton, Bill. *Giving: How Each of Us Can Change the World.* London: Hutchinson, 2007.

Clow, W. M. *Bible Reader's Encyclopædia and Concordance.* Rev. ed. New York: Collins' Clear-Type, 1962.

Collins, Jim. *Good to Great: Why Some Companies Make the Leap . . . And Others Don't.* New York: HarperCollins, 2011.

Collins, Jim and Jerry Porris. *Built to Last: Successful Habits of Visionary Companies.* Harper Collins. 1994.

Costello, Tim. *The Cost of Compassion.* Sydney: Acorn, 2020.

————. *Faith: Embracing Life in All Its Uncertainty.* Richmond, VIC: Hardie Grant, 2016.

————. *Hope.* Melbourne: Hardie Grant, 2012.

————. *A Lot with a Little.* Richmond, VIC: Hardie Grant, 2019.

————. *Ministry in an Urban World: Responding to the City.* Wanniassa, ACT: Acorn, 1991.

————. *Streets of Hope: Finding God in St Kilda.* Sydney: Allen & Unwin, 1997.

————. *Tips from a Travelling Soul-Searcher.* St. Leonards, NSW: Allen & Unwin, 1999.

Costello, Tim, and Royce Millar. *Wanna Bet? Winners and Losers in Gambling's Luck Myth.* Sydney: Allen & Unwin, 2000.

Covey, Stephen R. *The 7 Habits of Highly Effective People: Powerful Lessons in Personal Change.* New York: Simon & Schuster, 2013.

Dark, Eleanor. *Timeless Land.* Melbourne: Collins, 1942.

Department of Foreign Affairs and Trade. "Australia's Official Development Assistance Budget Summary 2023–24." https://www.dfat.gov.au/about-us/corporate/portfolio-budget-statements/australias-official-development-assistance-budget-summary-2023-24.

Encyclopedia Britannica. "William Carey." Last modified Aug. 13, 2025. https://www.britannica.com/biography/William-Carey.

Foundation Staff. "Krishnamurti's Biography." Krishnamurti Foundation Trust. https://kfoundation.org/krishnamurti-biography/.

Goleman, Daniel. *Emotional Intelligence: Why It Can Matter More Than IQ.* New York: Random House, 2005.

Greenleaf, Robert K. *The Servant as Leader.* Newton Center, MA: Greenleaf Center for Servant Leadership, 1973.

Hart, David Bentley. *Beauty of the Infinite: The Aesthetics of Christian Truth.* Grand Rapids: Eerdmans, 2003.

————. *The Experience of God: Being, Consciousness, Bliss.* New Haven: Yale University Press, 2013.

Henderson, Archibald. *George Bernard Shaw: His Life and Works; A Critical Biography.* Cincinnati: Stewart & Kidd, 1911.

Hickingbotham, Ian. *Waiting for the Tide.* Self-published, CreateSpace, 2013.

Holmes, Oliver Wendell. "The Voiceless." In *The Early Poems of Oliver Wendell Holmes,* 430. New York: Crowell, 1903. http://name.umdl.umich.edu/ACA8763.0001.001.

The Hunger Project. *"Yes We Can": Change Mindsets and Lives with the VCA Methodology.* Dec. 2020. https://www.thehungerproject.nl/wp-content/uploads/2021/02/Change-your-mindset-VCA-training-manual-The-Hunger-Project.pdf.

Jaworski, Joseph. *Synchronicity: The Inner Path of Leadership.* San Francisco: Berrett-Koehler, 2011.

Kennedy, John F. "Inaugural Address: January 20, 1961." In *Public Papers of the Presidents of the United States: John F. Kennedy, 1961,* 1. Washington, DC: US Government Printing Office, 1962.

Krishnamurti, Jiddu. *Think on These Things.* Edited by D. Rajagopal. New York: HarperPerennial, 1964.

———. *The First and Last Freedom.* Quest Book, Harper Row 1968.

Lewis, C. S. *Letters to Malcolm: Chiefly on Prayer.* San Diego: Harvest, 1964.

Markham, Edwin. *The Shoes of Happiness and Other Poems.* Garden City, NY: Doubleday, Page & Co., 1921.

Maslow, Abraham H. "A Theory of Human Motivation." *Psychological Review* 50 (1943) 370–96.

Murray, W. H. *The Scottish Himalayan Expedition.* London: Dent & Sons, 1951.

OECD. "Development Co-Operation Profiles: Australia." https://www.oecd.org/en/publications/development-co-operation-profiles_04b376d7-en/australia_b4d74d53-en.html.

Oxfam Australia. "About Us: Our History." https://www.oxfam.org.au/about-us/our-history/.

Parachin, Janet W. *Engaged Spirituality: Ten Lives of Contemplation and Action.* St. Louis: Chalice, 1999.

Peck, M. Scott. *The Different Drum: Community Making and Peace.* London: Arrow, 1990.

———. *The Road Less Traveled: A New Psychology of Love, Traditional Values and Spiritual Growth.* New York: Simon and Schuster, 2002.

Peterson, Jordan B. *12 Rules for Life: An Antidote to Chaos.* New York: Penguin, 2018.

Rumi, Jalal al-Din. *The Essential Rumi.* Translated by Coleman Barks. San Fransisco: Harper, 1995.

Senge, Peter. Introduction to *Synchronicity: The Inner Path of Leadership,* by Joseph Jaworski, edited by Betty Sue Flowers, 1–16. San Francisco: Berrett–Koehler, 2011.

Serampore Municipality. "Sir William Carey: The Father of Modern Missions in the East." https://seramporemunicipality.com/history_william_carry.php.

Shaw, George Bernard. *Man and Superman: A Comedy and a Philosophy.* London: Constable & Co., 1916.

Smith, George. *The Life of William Carey: Shoemaker and Missionary.* London: Dent & Sons, 1913.

Sojourners. "History of Sojourners." https://sojo.net/about-us/our-history.

Suzuki, David. *The Sacred Balance: Rediscovering Our Place in Nature.* Vancouver: Douglas & McIntyre, 2007.

Thoreau, Henry David. *Walden: A Writer's Edition.* Edited by Larzer Ziff. New York: Holt, Rinehart & Winston, 1961.

Tolle, Eckhart. *The Power of Now: A Guide to Spiritual Enlightenment.* Sydney: Hodder Headline Australia, 2000.

Tutu, Desmond. "The Longford Lecture: The Truth and Reconciliation Process—Restorative Justice." *Independent,* Feb. 16, 2004. https://www.independent.co.uk/voices/commentators/archbishop-desmond-tutu-the-longford-lecture-69546.html.

UNICEF. "Under-Five Mortality." Last updated Mar. 2025. https://data.unicef.org/topic/child-survival/under-five-mortality/.

United Nations. *The Justice and Reconciliation Process in Rwanda.* New York: Department of Public Information, 2014. https://www.un.org/en/preventgenocide/rwanda/assets/pdf/Backgrounder%20Justice%202014.pdf.

———. "Millennium Development Goals." https://www.un.org/millenniumgoals/.

———. "The 17 Goals." Department of Economic and Social Affairs. https://sdgs.un.org/goals.

———. "Transforming Our World: The 2030 Agenda for Sustainable Development." Department of Economic and Social Affairs, 2015. https://sdgs.un.org/2030agenda.

United Nations Development Programme. "1.1 Billion People Live in Multi-Dimensional Poverty, Nearly Half a Billion of These Live in Conflict Settings." Oct. 17, 2024. https://www.undp.org/press-releases/11-billion-people-live-multidimensional-poverty-nearly-half-billion-these-live-conflict-settings.

Vatican II. *Gaudium et Spes* (Pastoral Constitution on the Church in the Modern World). Vatican City: Libreria Editrice Vaticana, 1965.

Von Harten, Marjorie. *Walking in the World.* North Yorkshire: Coombe Springs, 1978.

Wallis, Jim. *Seven Ways to Change the World: Reviving Faith and Politics.* Oxford: Lion, 2008.

Williamson, Marianne. *A Return to Love: Reflections on the Principles of a Course in Miracles.* San Francisco: HarperOne, 1996.

World Bank Group. "Our Work." Institute for Economic Development. https://www.wbginstitute.org/about.

———. "Poverty." Last updated Oct. 2, 2025. https://www.worldbank.org/en/topic/poverty/overview.

———. "WBG Young Professionals Program (YPP): About the Program." https://www.worldbank.org/en/about/careers/the-young-professionals-program/aboutypp.

World Vision Australia. "About Us." https://www.wvi.org/about-us-9.

———. *2024 Annual Report: An Incredible Year of Australian Giving.* Burwood East, VIC: World Vision Australia, 2025. https://www.worldvision.com.au/docs/default-source/annual-reports/wv-annual-reports/world-vision-australia-annual-report-2024.pdf.

World Vision International. *Citizen Voice and Action: Civic Demand for Better Health and Education Services.* https://www.wvi.org/sites/default/files/CVA-Civic_Demand_for_Better_Health_and_Education_Services.pdf.

Wright, Alan, et al. *Engaged Spirituality: Prayer with the Providence of God.* 2015. https://www.wvi.org/sites/default/files/CVA%20A%20Spiritual%20Journey%20Part%201%20.pdf.

97